Getting Started with WebRTC

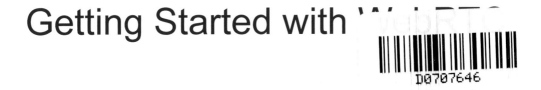

Explore WebRTC for real-time peer-to-peer communication

Rob Manson

[PACKT] PUBLISHING

open source*
community experience distilled

BIRMINGHAM - MUMBAI

Getting Started with WebRTC

Copyright © 2013 Packt Publishing

First published: September 2013

Production Reference: 1180913

Published by Packt Publishing Ltd.
Livery Place
35 Livery Street
Birmingham B3 2PB, UK..

ISBN 978-1-78216-630-6

www.packtpub.com

Cover Image by Suresh Mogre (suresh.mogre.99@gmail.com)

Credits

Author
Rob Manson

Reviewers
Todd Hunter
Alexandra Young

Acquisition Editor
Akram Hussain

Commissioning Editor
Shaon Basu

Technical Editors
Pratik More
Anusri Ramchandran

Project Coordinator
Akash Poojary

Proofreader
Clyde Jenkins

Indexers
Hemangini Bari
Mariammal Chettiyar

Graphics
Ronak Dhruv

Production Coordinator
Prachali Bhiwandkar

Cover Work
Prachali Bhiwandkar

About the Author

Rob Manson is the CEO and co-founder of *buildAR.com*, the world's leading Augmented Reality Content Management System. Rob is the Chairman of the W3C Augmented Web Community Group, and an Invited Expert with the ISO, W3C, and the Khronos Group. He is one of the co-founders of *ARStandards.org* and is an active evangelist within the global AR and standards communities. He is regularly invited to speak on the topics of the Augmented Web, Augmented Reality, WebRTC, and multi-device platforms.

I'd like to thank Alex, my wife and business partner—yes that's as crazy as it sounds! She's a great inspiration and always happy to put up with my creative ideas for using new technologies. She makes both my ideas and me as a person better in every way. I'd also like to thank Maggie and Todd for providing feedback and working with me on all our Multi-Device, WebRTC, and Augmented Web projects. I'm constantly amazed by just how much our team can achieve and you guys are the backbone that make this happen. I'm proud to say I work with you both.

About the Reviewers

Todd Hunter is a software developer with over 10 years experience of developing applications in a variety of industries. He is crazy enough to find his niche building interesting things with Perl, but with an eye for building things with the latest technologies. He has spent time in a wide range of companies, from the big multinationals to the smallest startups in industries ranging from large software companies, finance, to small high tech startups. He has a Bachelor's degree in Technology (Hons) and a Bachelor's degree in Applied Economics. He has a serious caffeine addiction.

Alexandra Young has been an innovator in User Experience across emerging technologies since the mid-90s. She led a team of designers and developers for one of Australia's largest telecommunications companies, responsible for defining the way in which people used products across Interactive TV, online, and mobile. For the last 6 years, Alex has worked on defining multi-device experiences for MOB (the research and development technology company she co-founded) on MOB's products, and complex platform developments for Enterprise, Government, and Cultural organizations. She is also an advocate for the Augmented Web, of which WebRTC is a critical component. Alex also speaks regularly at conferences on Augmented Reality, Mobile and Web Technologies, and User Experience.

Alexandra Young
CXO (Chief Experience Officer)
MOB-labs

www.PacktPub.com

Support files, eBooks, discount offers and more

You might want to visit www.PacktPub.com for support files and downloads related to your book.

Did you know that Packt offers eBook versions of every book published, with PDF and ePub files available? You can upgrade to the eBook version at www.PacktPub.com and as a print book customer, you are entitled to a discount on the eBook copy. Get in touch with us at service@packtpub.com for more details.

At www.PacktPub.com, you can also read a collection of free technical articles, sign up for a range of free newsletters and receive exclusive discounts and offers on Packt books and eBooks.

http://PacktLib.PacktPub.com

Do you need instant solutions to your IT questions? PacktLib is Packt's online digital book library. Here, you can access, read and search across Packt's entire library of books.

Why Subscribe?

- Fully searchable across every book published by Packt
- Copy and paste, print and bookmark content
- On demand and accessible via web browser

Free Access for Packt account holders

If you have an account with Packt at www.PacktPub.com, you can use this to access PacktLib today and view nine entirely free books. Simply use your login credentials for immediate access.

Table of Contents

Preface

Getting Started with WebRTC provides all the practical information you need to quickly understand what WebRTC is, how it works, and how you can add it to your own web applications. It includes clear working examples designed to help you get started with building WebRTC-enabled applications right away.

WebRTC delivers Web-based Real-Time Communication, and it is set to revolutionize our view of what the "Web" really is. The ability to stream audio and video from browser to browser alone is a significant innovation that will have far reaching implications for the telephony and video conferencing industries. But this is just the start. Opening raw access to the camera and microphone for JavaScript developers is already creating a whole new dynamic web that allows applications to interact with users through voice, gesture, and all kinds of new options.

On top of that, WebRTC also introduces real-time data channels that will allow interaction with dynamic data feeds from sensors and other devices. This really is a great time to be a web developer! However, WebRTC can also be quite daunting to get started with and many of its concepts can be new or a little confusing for even the most experienced web developers.

It's also important to understand that WebRTC is not really a single technology, but more a collection of standards and protocols, and it is still undergoing active evolution. The examples covered in this book are based on the latest version of the pre-1.0 version of the WebRTC standards at the time of writing. However, there are some areas of these standards that are under active debates and may change over the next year. The first is the way that the Session Description Protocol is integrated into the WebRTC call management process. The second is the general use of the overall offer/answer model that underlies the call setup process. And finally, there is also a strong push for the WebRTC standards to integrate the new Promise (previously known as Futures) design pattern. This all shows that this is a cutting edge, active, and exciting technology area, and that now is a great time to get involved as it grows and evolves.

We hope you appreciate this practical guide and that it makes it easy for you to get started with adding WebRTC to your applications right away.

What this book covers

Chapter 1, An Introduction to Web-based Real-Time Communication, introduces you to the concepts behind the new Web-based Real-Time Communication (WebRTC) standards.

Chapter 2, A More Technical Introduction to Web-based Real-Time Communication, takes you to the technical concepts behind the new Web-based Real-Time Communication (WebRTC) standards.

Chapter 3, Creating a Real-time Video Call, shows you how to use the MediaStream and RTCPeerConnection APIs to create a working peer-to-peer video chat application between two people.

Chapter 4, Creating an Audio Only Call, teaches you how to turn the video chat application we developed in the previous chapter into an audio only call application.

Chapter 5, Adding Text-based Chat, explains how to extend the video chat application we developed in *Chapter 2, A More Technical Introduction to Web-based Real-Time Communication,* to add support for text-based chat between the two users.

Chapter 6, Adding File Sharing, deals with how to extend the video chat application we developed in *Chapter 2, A More Technical Introduction to Web-based Real-Time Communication* and *Chapter 4, Creating an Audio Only Call*, to add support for file sharing between the two users.

Chapter 7, Example Application 1 — Education and E-learning, maps out what is involved in introducing WebRTC into e-learning applications.

Chapter 8, Example Application 2 — Team Communication, shows what is involved in introducing WebRTC into team your communication applications.

What you need for this book

All you need is:

- A text editor for creating HTML and JavaScript files
- A computer or server on which you can install Node.js (see instructions in *Chapter 2, A More Technical Introduction to Web-based Real-Time Communication*)
- One or more WebRTC capable web browsers (see instructions in *Chapter 1, An Introduction to Web-based Real-Time Communication*)

Who this book is for

Getting Started with WebRTC is written for web developers with moderate JavaScript experience who are interested in adding sensor driven real-time, peer-to-peer communication to their web applications.

Conventions

In this book, you will find a number of styles of text that distinguish among different kinds of information. Here are some examples of these styles, and an explanation of their meaning:

Code words in text are shown as follows:

"We can include other contexts through the use of the include directive."

A block of code is set as follows:

```
var page = undefined;
fs.readFile("basic_video_call.html", function(error, data) {
  if (error) {
    log_error(error);
  } else {
    page = data;
  }
});
```

When we wish to draw your attention to a particular part of a code block, the relevant lines or items are set in bold:

```
function setup_audio() {
  get_user_media(
    {
      "audio": true, // request access to local microphone
      "video": false  // don't request access to local camera
    },
    function (local_stream) { // success callback
      ...
    },
    log_error // error callback
  );
}
```

Any command-line input or output is written as follows:

```
#  node webrtc_signal_server.js
```

New terms and **important words** are shown in bold.

Reader feedback

Feedback from our readers is always welcome. Let us know what you think about this book—what you liked or may have disliked. Reader feedback is important for us to develop titles that you really find useful.

To send us general feedback, simply send an e-mail to feedback@packtpub.com, and mention the book title via the subject of your message.

If there is a topic in which you have expertise, and you are interested in either writing or contributing to a book, see our author guide on www.packtpub.com/authors.

Customer support

Now that you are the proud owner of a Packt book, we have a number of things to help you to get the most from your purchase.

Downloading the example code

You can download the example code files for all Packt books you have purchased from your account at http://www.packtpub.com. If you purchased this book elsewhere, you can visit http://www.packtpub.com/support and register to have the files e-mailed directly to you.

Errata

Although we have taken every care to ensure the accuracy of our content, mistakes do happen. If you find a mistake in one of our books—maybe a mistake in the text or the code—we would be grateful if you would report this to us. By doing so, you can save other readers from frustration and help us improve subsequent versions of this book. If you find any errata, please report them by visiting http://www.packtpub. com/submit-errata, selecting your book, clicking on the **errata submission form** link, and entering the details of your errata. Once your errata are verified, your submission will be accepted and the errata will be uploaded on our website, or added to any list of existing errata, under the Errata section of that title. Any existing errata can be viewed by selecting your title from http://www.packtpub.com/support.

Piracy

Piracy of copyright material on the Internet is an ongoing problem across all media. At Packt, we take the protection of our copyright and licenses very seriously. If you come across any illegal copies of our works, in any form, on the Internet, please provide us with the location address or website name immediately so that we can pursue a remedy.

Please contact us at copyright@packtpub.com with a link to the suspected pirated material.

We appreciate your help in protecting our authors, and our ability to bring you valuable content.

Questions

You can contact us at questions@packtpub.com if you are having a problem with any aspect of the book, and we will do our best to address it.

1
An Introduction to Web-based Real-Time Communication

This chapter introduces you to the concepts behind the new **Web-based Real-Time Communication (WebRTC)** standards. After reading this chapter, you will have a clear understanding of:

- What is WebRTC
- How you can use it
- Which web browsers support it

Introducing WebRTC

When the **World Wide Web (WWW)** was first created in the early 1990's, it was built upon a page-centric model that used HREF-based hyperlinks. In this early model of the web, browsers navigated from one page to another in order to present new content and to update their HTML-based user interfaces.

Around the year 2000, a new approach to web browsing had started to develop, and by the middle of that decade, it had become standardized as the **XMLHttpRequest (XHR)** API. This new XHR API enabled web developers to create web applications that didn't need to navigate to a new page to update their content or user interface. It allowed them to utilize server-based web services that provided access to structured data and snippets of pages or other content. This led to a whole new approach to the web, which is now commonly referred to as Web 2.0. The introduction of this new XHR API enabled services such as Gmail, Facebook, Twitter, and more to create a much more dynamic and social web for us.

Now the web is undergoing yet another transformation that enables individual web browsers to stream data directly to each other without the need for sending it via intermediary servers. This new form of peer-to-peer communication is built upon a new set of APIs that is being standardized by the *Web Real-Time Communications Working Group* available at `http://www.w3.org/2011/04/webrtc/` of the **World Wide Web Consortium** (**W3C**), and a set of protocols standardized by *Real-Time Communication in WEB-browsers* Working Group available at `http://tools.ietf.org/wg/rtcweb/` of the **Internet Engineering Task Force** (**IETF**).

Just as the introduction of the XHR API led to the Web 2.0 revolution, the introduction of the new WebRTC standards is creating a new revolution too.

It's time to say hello to the real-time web!

Uses for WebRTC

The real-time web allows you to set up dynamic connections to other web browsers and web-enabled devices quickly and easily. This opens the door to a whole new range of peer-to-peer communication, including text-based chat, file sharing, screen sharing, gaming, sensor data feeds, audio calls, video chat, and more. You can now see that the implications of WebRTC are very broad. Direct and secure peer-to-peer communication between browsers will have a big impact on the modern web, reshaping the way we use the physical networks that make up the Internet.

Direct peer-to-peer connections often provide lower latency, making gaming, video streaming, sensor data feeds, and so on, appear faster and more interactive or real-time, hence the use of this term.

Secure peer-to-peer connections allow you to exchange information privately without it being logged or managed by intermediary servers. This reduces the need for some large service providers while creating opportunities for people to create new types of services and applications. It introduces improved privacy for some individuals while it may also create new complexities for regulators and law enforcement organizations.

And the efficient peer-to-peer exchange of binary data streams removes the need to serialize, re-encode, or convert this data at each step in the process. This leads to a much more efficient use of network and application resources, as well as creating a less error prone and more robust data exchange pipeline.

This is just a brief overview of how you can use WebRTC, and by the end of this book, you will have all the information you need to start turning your own new ideas into practical applications.

Try WebRTC yourself right now!

The goal of this book is to get you started with WebRTC, so let's do that right now. You can easily find out if your browser supports the camera access functionality by visiting one of the existing demo sites such as http://www.simpl.info/getusermedia, and if it does, you should be prompted to provide permission to share your camera. Once you provide this permission, you should see a web page with a live video stream from your PC or mobile devices' video camera, and be experiencing the interesting sensation of looking at a video of yourself staring right back at you. That's how simple it is to start using WebRTC.

Now, perhaps you'd like to try using it to communicate with another person. You can do this by visiting another demo site such as http://apprtc.appspot.com, which will create a unique URL for your video chat. Just send this URL to another person with a browser that also supports WebRTC, and once they open that page, you should see two video elements displayed on the page: one from your local video camera and one from the other person's video camera. There's a lot of complex negotiation that's gone on in the background, but assuming your browser supports WebRTC and your network doesn't actively prevent it, then you should now have a clear idea of just how easy it is to use.

But what web browsers support WebRTC? Let's find out.

Browser compatibility

The WebRTC standards landscape is home to one of the fastest evolving communities on the web. One of the biggest challenges this creates is that of compatibility and interoperability. Here is an overview of what this is up to today and how to stay up-to-date as this continues to evolve.

Chrome and Firefox on the PC

At the time this chapter was written, WebRTC was supported as default by Chrome and Firefox on mainstream PC Operating Systems such as Mac OS X, Windows, and Linux. And most importantly, these two key implementations have been shown to communicate well with each other through a range of interoperability tests.

 Have a look at the *Hello Chrome, it's Firefox calling!* blog post at https://hacks.mozilla.org/2013/02/hello-chrome-its-firefox-calling/.

Chrome and Firefox on Android

WebRTC is also available for Chrome and Firefox on the Android platform; however, currently you must manually configure certain settings to enable this functionality.

Here are the key steps you need to enable this for Chrome. These are from the Chrome for Android release notes posted on the *discuss-webrtc* forum available at `https://groups.google.com/forum/#!topic/discuss-webrtc/uFOMhd-AG0A`:

To enable WebRTC on Chrome for Android:

1. Type in `chrome://flags/` in the omnibox to access the flags.
2. Scroll about a third down and enable the **Enable WebRTC** flag.
3. You will be asked to relaunch the browser at the bottom of the page in order for the flag to take effect.

Enabling WebRTC using Chrome flags on Android

Here are the key steps you need to enable WebRTC for Firefox. These are from a post on the Mozilla Hacks blog about the new Firefox for Android release available at `https://hacks.mozilla.org/2013/04/webrtc-update-our-first-implementation-will-be-in-release-soon-welcome-to-the-party-but-please-watch-your-head/`:

> *You can enable it by setting both the media.navigator.enabled pref and the media.peerconnection.enabled pref to "true" (browse to about:config and search for media.navigator.enabled and media.peerconnection.enabled in the list of prefs).*

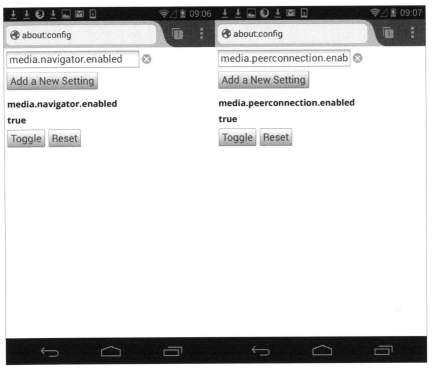

Enabling WebRTC using Firefox settings on Android

Opera

Opera has been an active supporter of the WebRTC movement and has implemented early versions of this standard in previous releases of their browsers. But at the time this chapter was written, they were working to port their collection of browsers to the **WebKit** platform based on the open **Chromium** project. So, until this migration activity is complete, their support for WebRTC is currently listed as unavailable.

However, since the Chromium project is closely related to Chrome, which is also built upon the WebKit platform, it is expected that Opera's support for WebRTC will develop quickly after this migration is complete.

Microsoft

Microsoft has proposed its own alternative to WebRTC named **Customizable, Ubiquitous Real-Time Communication over the Web (CU-RTC-Web)**. Have a look at `http://html5labs.interoperabilitybridges.com/cu-rtc-web/cu-rtc-web.htm`.

As yet, it has not announced any timeline as to when Internet Explorer may support WebRTC, but it is currently possible to use WebRTC within Internet Explorer using the Chrome Frame solution available at `https://developers.google.com/chrome/chrome-frame/`.

Microsoft has also recently released prototypes that show interoperability in the form of a voice chat application connecting Chrome on a Mac and IE10 on Windows available at `http://blogs.msdn.com/b/interoperability/archive/2013/01/17/ms-open-tech-publishes-html5-labs-prototype-of-a-customizable-ubiquitous-real-time-communication-over-the-web-api-proposal.aspx`. This shows that one way or another, Microsoft understands the significance of the WebRTC movement, and it is actively engaging in the standards discussions.

Apple

Apple has not yet made any announcement about when they plan to support WebRTC in **Safari** on either OS X or iOS. So far, the only application that has made WebRTC available on iOS is an early proof of concept browser created by Ericsson Labs named **Bowser**, and is available at `http://labs.ericsson.com/apps/bowser`.

Bowser is based upon a very early experimental version of the WebRTC standards, and it does not interoperate with any of the other mainstream web browsers.

However, as Safari is also based upon the WebKit platform just like Chrome and Opera, there should be no major technical barriers to prevent Apple from enabling WebRTC on both their mobile and PC browsers.

Staying up-to-date

It is also important to note that WebRTC is not a single API, but really a collection of APIs and protocols defined by a variety of Working Groups, and that the support for each of these are developing at different rates on different browsers and operating systems.

A great way to see where the latest level of support has reached is through services such as `http://caniuse.com`, which tracks broad adoption of modern APIs across multiple browsers and operating systems.

And, you should also check out the open project at `http://www.webrtc.org`, which is supported by Google, Mozilla, and Opera. This project provides a set of C++ libraries that are designed to help browser and application developers quickly and easily implement standards compliant with WebRTC functionality. It is also a useful site to find the latest information on browser support and some great WebRTC demos.

Summary

You should now have a clear overview of what the term WebRTC means and for what it can be used. You should be able to identify which browsers support WebRTC and have all the resources you need to find the latest up-to-date information on how this is evolving. You should also have been able to try the different aspects of WebRTC for yourself quickly and easily using your own browser if you so choose.

Next, we will take a more technical look at how the different WebRTC API components all fit together.

Then, we will start by fleshing out the simple peer-to-peer video call scenario into a fully working application.

Later, we will explore how this can be simplified down to just an audio only call or extended with text-based chat and file sharing.

And then, we will explore two real-world application scenarios based upon e-learning and team communication.

2
A More Technical Introduction to Web-based Real-Time Communication

This chapter introduces you to the technical concepts behind the new **Web-based Real-Time Communication (WebRTC)** standards. After reading this chapter, you will have a clear understanding of the following topics:

- How to set up peer-to-peer communication
- The signaling options available
- How the key APIs relate to each other

Setting up communication

Although the basis of WebRTC communication is peer-to-peer, the initial step of setting up this communication requires some sort of coordination. This is most commonly provided by a web server and/or a signaling server. This enables two or more WebRTC capable devices or peers to find each other, exchange contact details, negotiate a session that defines how they will communicate, and then finally establish the direct peer-to-peer streams of media that flows between them.

The general flow

There are a wide range of scenarios, ranging from single web page demos running on a single device to complex distributed multi-party conferencing with a combination of media relays and archiving services. To get started, we will focus on the most common flow, which covers two web browsers using WebRTC to set up a simple video call between them.

Following is the summary of this flow:

- Connect users
- Start signals
- Find candidates
- Negotiate media sessions
- Start RTCPeerConnection streams

Connect users

The very first step in this process is for the two users to connect in some way. The simplest option is that both the users visit the same website. This page can then identify each browser and connect both of them to a shared signaling server, using something like the WebSocket API. This type of web page, often, assigns a unique token that can be used to link the communication between these two browsers. You can think of this token as a room or conversation ID. In the `http://apprtc.appspot.com` demo described previously, the first user visits `http://apprtc.appspot.com`, and is then provided with a unique URL that includes a new unique token. This first user then sends this unique URL to the second user, and once they both have this page open at the same time the first step is complete.

Start signals

Now that both users have a shared token, they can now exchange signaling messages to negotiate the setup of their WebRTC connection. In this context, "signaling messages" are simply any form of communication that helps these two browsers establish and control their WebRTC communication. The WebRTC standards don't define exactly how this has to be completed. This is a benefit, because it leaves this part of the process open for innovation and evolution. It is also a challenge as this uncertainty often confuses developers who are new to RTC communication in general. The apprtc demo described previously uses a combination of XHR and the Google AppEngine Channel API (`https://developers.google.com/appengine/docs/python/channel/overview`). This could, just as easily, be any other approach such as XHR polling, Server-Sent Events (`http://www.html5rocks.com/en/tutorials/eventsource/basics/`), WebSockets (`http://www.html5rocks.com/en/tutorials/websockets/basics/`), or any combination of these, you feel comfortable with.

Find candidates

The next step is for the two browsers to exchange information about their networks, and how they can be contacted. This process is commonly described as "finding candidates", and at the end each browser should be mapped to a directly accessible network interface and port. Each browser is likely to be sitting behind a router that may be using Network Address Translation (NAT) to connect the local network to the internet. Their routers may also impose firewall restrictions that block certain ports and incoming connections. Finding a way to connect through these types of routers is commonly known as NAT Traversal (`http://en.wikipedia.org/wiki/NAT_traversal`), and is critical for establishing a WebRTC communication. A common way to achieve this is to use a Session Traversal Utilities for NAT (STUN) server (`http://en.wikipedia.org/wiki/Session_Traversal_Utilities_for_NAT`), which simply helps to identify how you can be contacted from the public internet and then returns this information in a useful form. There are a range of people that provide public STUN servers. The apprtc demo previously described uses one provided by Google.

If the STUN server cannot find a way to connect to your browser from the public internet, you are left with no other option than to fall back to using a solution that relays your media, such as a Traversal Using Relay NAT (TURN) server (`http://en.wikipedia.org/wiki/Traversal_Using_Relay_NAT`). This effectively takes you back to a non peer-to-peer architecture, but in some cases, where you are inside a particularly strict private network, this may be your only option.

Within WebRTC, this whole process is usually bound into a single Interactive Connectivity Establishment (ICE) framework (`http://en.wikipedia.org/wiki/Interactive_Connectivity_Establishment`) that handles connecting to a STUN server and then falling back to a TURN server where required.

Negotiate media sessions

Now that both the browsers know how to talk to each other, they must also agree on the type and format of media (for example, audio and video) they will exchange including codec, resolution, bitrate, and so on. This is usually negotiated using an offer/answer based model, built upon the Session Description Protocol (**SDP**) (`http://en.wikipedia.org/wiki/Session_Description_Protocol`). This has been defined as the JavaScript Session Establishment Protocol (**JSEP**); for more information visit `http://tools.ietf.org/html/draft-ietf-rtcweb-jsep-00)` by the IETF.

Start RTCPeerConnection streams

Once this has all been completed, the browsers can finally start streaming media to each other, either directly through their peer-to-peer connections or via any media relay gateway they have fallen back to using.

At this stage, the browsers can continue to use the same signaling server solution for sharing communication to control this WebRTC communication. They can also use a specific type of WebRTC data channel to do this directly with each other.

Using WebSockets

The WebSocket API makes it easy for web developers to utilize bidirectional communication within their web applications. You simply create a new connection using the `var connection = new WebSocket(url);` constructor, and then create your own functions to handle when messages and errors are received. And sending a message is as simple as using the `connection.send(message);` method.

The key benefit here is that the messaging is truly bidirectional, fast, and lightweight. This means the WebSocket API server can send messages directly to your browser whenever it wants, and you receive them as soon as they happen. There are no delays or constant network traffic as it is in the XHR polling or long-polling model, which makes this ideal for the sort of offer/answer signaling dance that's required to set up WebRTC communication.

The WebSocket API server can then use the unique room or conversation token, previously described, to work out which of the WebSocket API clients messages should be relayed to. In this manner, a single WebSocket API server can support a very large number of clients. And since the network connection setup happens very rarely, and the messages themselves tend to be small, the server resources required are very modest.

There are WebSocket API libraries available in almost all major programming languages, and since `Node.js` is based on JavaScript, it has become a popular choice for this type of implementation. Libraries such as `socket.io` (`http://socket.io/`) provide a great example of just how easy this approach can really be.

Other signaling options

Any approach that allows browsers to send and receive messages via a server can be used for WebRTC signaling.

The simplest model is to use the XHR API to send messages and to poll the server periodically to collect any new messages. This can be easily implemented by any web developer without any additional tools. However, it has a number of drawbacks. It has a built-in delay based on the frequency of each polling cycle. It is also a waste of bandwidth, as the polling cycle is repeated even when no messages are ready to be sent or received. But if you're looking for a good old-fashioned solution, then this is the one.

A slightly more refined approach based on polling is called long-polling. In this model, if the server doesn't have any new messages yet, the network connection is kept alive until it does, using the HTTP 1.1 keep-alive mechanisms. When the server has some new information, it just sends it down the wire to complete the request. In this case, the network overhead of the polling is reduced. But it is still an outdated and inefficient approach compared to more modern solutions such as WebSockets.

Server-Sent Events are another option. You establish a connection to the server using the `var source = new EventSource(url);` constructor, and then add listeners to that `source` object to handle messages sent by the server. This allows servers to send you messages directly, and you receive them as soon as they happen. But you are still left using a separate channel, such as XHR, to send your messages to the server, which means you are forced to manage and synchronize two separate channels. This combination does provide a useful solution that has been used in a number of WebRTC demonstration apps, but it does not have the same elegance as a truly bidirectional channel, such as WebSockets.

There are all kinds of other creative ideas that could be used to facilitate the required signaling as well. But what we have covered are the most common options you will find being used.

MediaStream API

The **MediaStream** API is designed to allow you to access streams of media from local input devices, such as cameras and microphones. It was initially focused upon the **getUserMedia** API or **gUM** for short, but has now been formalized as the broader media capture and streams API, or MediaStream API for short. However, the `getUserMedia()` method is still the primary way to initiate access to local input devices.

Each MediaStream object can contain a number of different MediaStreamTrack objects that each represents different input media, such as video or audio from different input sources.

Each MediaStreamTrack can then contain multiple channels (for example, the left and right audio channels). These channels are the smallest units that are defined by the MediaStream API.

MediaStream objects can then be output in two key ways. First, they can be used to render output into a **MediaElement** such as a `<video>` or `<audio>` element (although the latter may require pre-processing). Secondly, they can be used to send to an **RTCPeerConnection**, which can then send this media stream to a remote peer.

Each MediaStreamTrack can be represented in a number of states described by the `MediaSourceStates` object returned by the `states()` method. Each MediaStreamTrack can also provide a range of capabilities, which can be accessed through the `capabilities()` method.

At the top level, a MediaStream object can fire a range of events such as `addtrack`, `removetrack`, or `ended`. And below that a MediaStreamTrack can fire a range of events such as `started`, `mute`, `unmute`, `overconstrainted`, and `ended`.

RTCPeerConnection API

The RTCPeerConnection API is the heart of the peer-to-peer connection between each of the WebRTC enabled browsers or peers. To create an RTCPeerConnection object, you use the `var peerconnection = RTCPeerConnection(configuration);` constructor. The `configuration` variable contains at least one key named `iceServers`, which is an array of URL objects that contain information about STUN, and possibly TURN servers, used during the finding candidates phase.

The `peerconnection` object is then used in slightly different ways on each client, depending upon whether you are the caller or the callee.

The caller's flow

Here's a summary of the caller's flow after the `peerconnection` object is created:

- Register the `onicecandidate` handler
- Register the `onaddstream` handler
- Register the `message` handler
- Use getUserMedia to access the local camera
- The JSEP offer/answer process

Register the onicecandidate handler

First, you register an `onicecandidate` handler that sends any ICE candidates to the other peer, as they are received using one of the signaling channels described previously.

Register the onaddstream handler

Then, you register an `onaddstream` handler that displays the video stream once it is received from the remote peer.

Register the message handler

Your signaling channel should also have a handler registered that responds to messages received from the other peer. If the message contains an `RTCIceCandidate` object, it should add those to the `peerconnection` object using the `addIceCandidate()` method. And if the message contains an `RTCSessionDescription` object, it should add those to the `peerconnection` object using the `setRemoteDescription()` method.

Use getUserMedia to access the local camera

Then, you can utilize `getUserMedia()` to set up your local media stream and display that on your local page, and also add it to the `peerconnection` object using the `addStream()` method.

The JSEP offer/answer process

Now, you are ready to start the negotiation using the `createOffer()` method and registering a callback handler that receives an `RTCSessionDescription` object. This callback handler should then add this `RTCSessionDescription` to your `peerconnection` object using `setLocalDescription()`. And then finally, it should also send this `RTCSessionDescription` to the remote peer through your signaling channel.

The callee's flow

The following is a summary of the callee's flow, which is very similar in a lot of ways to the caller's flow, except that it responds to the offer with an answer:

- Register the `onicecandidate` handler
- Register the `onaddstream` handler

- Register the `message` handler
- Use getUserMedia to access the local camera
- The JSEP offer/answer process

Register the onicecandidate handler

Just like the caller, you start by registering an `onicecandidate` handler that sends any ICE candidates to the other peer as they are received, using one of the signaling channels described previously.

Register the onaddstream handler

Then, like the caller, you register an `onaddstream` handler that displays the video stream once it is received from the remote peer.

Register the message handler

Like the caller, your signaling channel should also have a handler registered that responds to messages received from the other peer. If the message contains an `RTCIceCandidate` object, it should add those to the `peerconnection` object using the `addIceCandidate()` method. And if the message contains an `RTCSessionDescription` object, it should add those to the `peerconnection` object using the `setRemoteDescription()` method.

Use getUserMedia to access the local camera

Then, like the caller, you can utilize `getUserMedia()` to set up your local media stream and display that on your local page, and also add it to the `peerconnection` object using the `addStream()` method.

The JSEP offer/answer process

Here you differ from the caller and you play your part in the negotiation by passing `remoteDescription` to the `createAnswer()` method and registering a callback handler that receives an `RTCSessionDescription` object. This callback handler should then add this `RTCSessionDescription` to your `peerconnection` object using `setLocalDescription()`. And then finally, it should also send this `RTCSessionDescription` to the remote peer through your signaling channel. It is also important to note that this callee flow is all initiated after the offer is received from the caller.

Where does RTCPeerConnection sit?

The following diagram shows the overall WebRTC architecture from the `www.WebRTC.org` site. It shows you the level of complexity that is hidden below the RTCPeerConnection API.

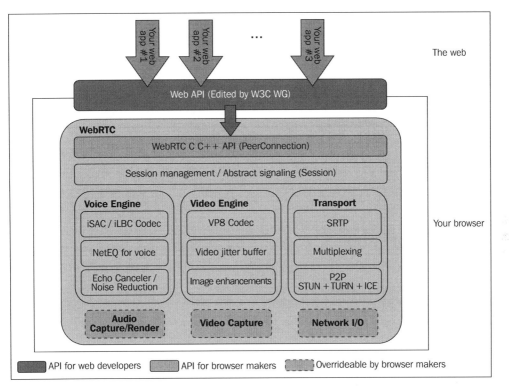

Overall architecture diagram from `www.WebRTC.org`

RTCDataChannel API

As well as sending media streams between peers using WebRTC, it is also possible to use the DataChannel API to send arbitrary streams of data. Although many people commonly refer to this as the RTCDataChannel API, it is more accurately defined as just the WebRTC DataChannel API and is created by using the `var datachannel = peerconnection.createDataChannel(label);` constructor. It is a very flexible and powerful solution that has been specifically designed to be similar to the WebSocket API through the `send()` method and the `onmessage` event.

At the time of writing this chapter, this API is still in a state of flux with the varying browser implementations still struggling with standardization.

Summary

You should now have a clear overview of the various APIs and protocols that combine to make WebRTC work.

Throughout the rest of the book, we will explore the MediaStream, RTCPeerConnection, and RTCDataChannel APIs in more detail as we work to apply these concepts to real world examples.

First, we will start by fleshing out the simple peer-to-peer video call scenario into a fully working application.

Then, we will explore how this can be simplified down to just an audio only call or extended with text-based chat and file sharing.

And then, we will explore two real-world application scenarios based upon e-learning and team communication.

3
Creating a Real-time Video Call

This chapter shows you how to use the MediaStream and RTCPeerConnection APIs to create a working peer-to-peer video chat application between two people. After reading this chapter, you will have a clear understanding of:

- Using a web server to connect two users
- Setting up a signaling server for a peer-to-peer call
- How the caller's browser creates an offer
- How the callee's browser responds with an answer
- Previewing local video streams
- Establishing and presenting remote video streams
- The types of stream processing available
- Extending this into a Chatroulette application

Setting up a simple WebRTC video call

The most common WebRTC example application involves setting up a video call between two separate users. Within a few seconds, you can easily see and talk to anyone, anywhere in the world who has one of the one billion or more WebRTC-enabled browsers. Let's take a detailed look at how this can be achieved and create the code we need as we go.

Throughout this book, some simple coding conventions will be used to aid communication and readability.

JavaScript APIs standardized by the W3C and other standards definition organizations will use the conventional camel case format (for example, `standardFunctionCall()`).

Functions and variables that have been defined for this book will use all lowercase strings and replace word breaks or white space with an underscore (for example, `custom_function_call()`).

The web and WebSocket server functionality in this example application will be implemented using JavaScript and Node.js. It is beyond the scope of this book to provide information on how to install and configure Node.js, but all the information you need can be found at `http://nodejs.org/`.

However, this book does provide you with well-described working Node.js example code that provides all the functionality you need to run the demonstration applications.

A basic peer-to-peer video call using WebRTC

Using a web server to connect two users

The very first step is simply to connect two separate users using the Web. We start by creating a standard HTML5 web page that includes a DOCTYPE definition, a document head, and a document body:

```
<!DOCTYPE html>
<html>
<head>
...
</head>
<body>
...
</body>
</html>
```

Downloading the example code

You can download the example code files for all Packt books you have purchased from your account at http://www.packtpub.com. If you purchased this book elsewhere, you can visit http://www.packtpub.com/support and register to have the files e-mailed directly to you.

Then, the first element inside the document head is the webrtc_polyfill.js script included inline between a pair of <script> tags. The webrtc_polyfill.js code is exactly what it says it is and is designed to make it easy to write JavaScript that works across all common browser implementations of the WebRTC and MediaStream APIs. Here is an overview of how it works.

First, we set up six global placeholders for the primary features it exposes:

```
var webrtc_capable = true;
var rtc_peer_connection = null;
var rtc_session_description = null;
var get_user_media = null;
var connect_stream_to_src = null;
var stun_server = "stun.l.google.com:19302";
```

These global placeholders are then populated with their final values, based on the type of browser capabilities that are detected.

rtc_peer_connection is a pointer to either the standard RTCPeerConnection, mozRTCPeerConnection if you are using an early Firefox WebRTC implementation, or webkitRTCPeerConnection if you are using an early WebRTC implementation in a WebKit-based browser like Chrome.

`rtc_session_description` is also a pointer to the browser-specific implementation of the `RTCSessionDescription` constructor. For this, the only real exception is within the early Firefox WebRTC implementation.

`get_user_media` is very similar. It is either a pointer to the standard `navigator.getUserMedia`, `navigator.mozGetUserMedia` if you are using an early MediaStream API implementation in Firefox, or `navigator.webkitUserMedia` if you are using an early MediaStream API implementation in a WebKit-based browser such as Chrome.

`connect_stream_to_src` is a function that accepts a reference to a MediaStream object and a reference to an HTML5 `<video>` media element. It then connects the stream to the `<video>` element so that it can be displayed within the local browser.

Finally, the `stun_server` variable holds a pointer to Google's public STUN server. Currently, Firefox requires this to be an IP address, but Chrome supports DNS-based hostnames and ports.

The heart of the browser detection is then handled in a set of simple `if/else` blocks.

First, it checks if the standard `navigator.getUserMedia` is supported, else it checks if `navigator.mozGetUserMedia` is supported (for example, early Firefox MediaStream API), or else if `navigator.webkitGetUserMedia` is supported (for example, an early WebKit browser MediaStream API).

The final else block then assumes that this is a browser that doesn't support `getUserMedia` at all. This code also assumes that if `getUserMedia` is supported in some way, then a matching RTCPeerConnection API is also implicitly supported.

The `connect_stream_to_src` function then is adapted slightly, based on which type of browser has been detected.

The default standard version directly assigns the `media_stream` to the video element's `.srcObject` property:

```
connect_stream_to_src = function(media_stream, media_element) {
  media_element.srcObject = media_stream;
  media_element.play();
};
```

Within the early Firefox WebRTC implementations, the `<video>` media element uses the `mozSrcObject` property, which can have the media stream object directly assigned to it:

```
connect_stream_to_src = function(media_stream, media_element) {
  media_element.mozSrcObject = media_stream;
  media_element.play();
};
```

Within the early WebKit-based WebRTC implementations, the `webkitURL.createObjectURL` function is passed the media stream object, and the response from this is then directly assigned to the `<video>` element's `.src` property:

```
connect_stream_to_src = function(media_stream, media_element) {
    media_element.src = webkitURL.createObjectURL(media_stream);
};
```

Once `webrtc_polyfill.js` has set up everything, we need to create browser independent WebRTC code; we can then move onto the body of this video call application. The code that defines the `basic_video_call.js` browser side logic for this is included inline within another pair of `<script></script>` tags.

First, we set up the general variables that we will use throughout the rest of the code.

The `call_token` variable is a unique ID that links two users together. It is used to ensure that any signals passing through the signaling server are only exchanged between these two specific users.

```
var call_token; // unique token for this call
```

The `signaling_server` is a variable that represents the WebSocket API connection to the signaling server to which both the caller and callee will be connected:

```
var signaling_server; // signaling server for this call
```

The `peer_connection` variable represents the actual RTCPeerConnection that will be established between these two users:

```
var peer_connection; // peerconnection object
```

Next, we set up a basic `start()` function that is called by the pages' `body.onload` event:

```
function start() {
```

This function essentially detects if you are the caller or the callee, and then sets up the relevant functionality to match. It also sets up a number of common functions that are used by both the caller and the callee.

The first step here is to populate the `peer_connection` variable with a real RTCPeerConnection object using the `rtc_peer_connection` constructor setup by `webrtc_polyfill.js`. We pass a configuration object to this function that defines the STUN server we would like to use. In this example, we have used a public STUN server provided by Google; however, this is for demonstration purposes only. If you intend to build a commercial application, you must find a commercial STUN provider.

```
// create the WebRTC peer connection object
peer_connection = new rtc_peer_connection({
    "iceServers": [
        { "url": "stun:"+stun_server }, // stun server info
    ]
});
```

Next, we set up our own function for the `peer_connection.onicecandidate` event handler and if `ice_event` contains a candidate then we serialize this into a JSON blob and send that to the other caller's browser through the `signaling_server` variable:

```
// generic handler that sends any ice candidates to the other peer
peer_connection.onicecandidate = function (ice_event) {
    ...
};
```

Then, we set up our own function for the `peer_connection.onaddstream` handler. This simply receives any new incoming video streams and connects them to a local `<video>` element within the local browser, so you can see and hear the person on the other end of the call.

```
// display remote video streams when they arrive
peer_connection.onaddstream = function (event) {
    ...
};
```

Later, we set up our connection to the signaling server using the WebSocket API. This is generic, because this same type of connection is used by both the caller and the callee. It is essential that both are connected to the same signaling server in this basic example.

```
// setup generic connection to the signaling server using the
WebSocket API
signaling_server = new WebSocket("ws://localhost:1234");
```

Now, all of the generic functionality has been set up, and we can move onto customizing the rest based on whether you are a caller or a callee. This is simply done by detecting whether the browser has loaded a page with a `call_token` hash fragment or not.

If you are the caller, then you are the first person to visit the page, and you will have no `call_token` at all. In this case, we will create one for you and set `location.hash` so that you can see this in your browser's location bar (for example, `http://localhost:1234#1370439693969-433`). It is important to note that `localhost` should be replaced with the hostname or IP address that you actually intend to use, and that this must also be accessible to the other person that intends to join the call.

You can then send this URL to the other person (via e-mail, SMS, carrier pigeon, or whatever method works best for you). Once they load this URL, we will then detect that they already have a `call_token` hash fragment defined and will then treat them as the callee.

```
if (document.location.hash === ""
   || document.location.hash === undefined) { // you are the Caller
   ...
} else { // you have a hash fragment so you must be the Callee
   ...
}
}
```

Following the `start()` function, we define the detailed implementation of a number of other generic handler functions that are used by either or both the caller and the callee.

First, we implement the function that handles any new descriptions that are set up in the JSEP offer/answer process. This will be described in more detail in the following code snippet:

```
// handler to process new descriptions
function new_description_created(description) {
   ...
}
```

Then, we implement the function that handles all the signals we receive from the signaling server from the perspective of the caller. This handles four key scenarios:

1. If `signal.type` is `callee_arrived`, then we start the JSEP offer/answer process. This is described in more detail in the code snippet that follows.

2. If `signal.type` is `new_ice_candidate`, then this candidate is added to `peer_connection`.

3. If signal.type is new_description, then we call peer_connection. setRemoteDescription().

4. Or else you can extend this with your own custom signaling.

Here is the function that handles these four scenarios:

```
// handle signals as a caller
function caller_signal_handler(event) {
    var signal = JSON.parse(event.data);
    if (signal.type === "callee_arrived") {
        ...
    } else if (signal.type === "new_ice_candidate") {
        ...
    } else if (signal.type === "new_description") {
        ...
    } else {
        // extend with your own signal types here
    }
}
```

Then, we implement the function that handles all the signals we receive from the signaling server from the perspective of the callee. This is similar to the caller function that we just saw, except it only handles 3 key scenarios:

1. If signal.type is new_ice_candidate, then this candidate is added to the peer_connection.

2. If signal.type is new_description, then we call peer_connection. setRemoteDescription(), and if the description contains an offer, then we create an answer.

3. Or else you can extend this with your own custom signaling.

Here is the function that handles these three scenarios:

```
// handle signals as a callee
function callee_signal_handler(event) {
    var signal = JSON.parse(event.data);
    if (signal.type === "new_ice_candidate") {
        ...
    } else if (signal.type === "new_description") {
        ...
    } else {
        // extend with your own signal types here
    }
}
```

Now, we implement the function that requests access to the local camera's video stream using the `getUserMedia` call. If this stream is set up successfully, then it is displayed on the local browser page in a `<video>` element and then added to the `peer_connection` object so that it can be sent to the remote peer's browser. If this local stream is not set up successfully, then the error is logged so that the user can be notified.

```
// setup stream from the local camera
function setup_video() {
   get_user_media(
      {
         "audio": true, // request access to local microphone
         "video": true  // request access to local camera
      },
      function (local_stream) { // success callback
         . . .
      },
      log_error // error callback
   );
}
```

Then, we define a generic error handler function that logs the error and notifies the user, so they know what has happened:

```
// generic error handler
function log_error(error) {
   ...
}
```

Once all of the JavaScript code has been defined, then we move on to defining some simple CSS based styles. You can obviously customize this as much as you like, but in this example, we have provided the basic styles you need to understand on how you can quickly and easily create a user interface that handles all of the different states required for this video call application.

First, we create a style for the `loading_state`, `open_call_state`, `local_video`, and `remote_video` ID's, and set them to not be displayed by default.

Then, we set the style for `loading_state` to make sure it is displayed by default. This content is shown to both the caller and the callee when they first load the page.

```
<style>
html, body {
   padding: 0px;
   margin: 0px;
   font-family: "Arial","Helvetica",sans-serif;
```

```
  }
  #loading_state {
    position: absolute;
    top: 45%;
    left: 0px;
    width: 100%;
    font-size: 20px;
    text-align: center;
  }
  #open_call_state {
    display: none;
  }
  #local_video {
    position: absolute;
    top: 10px;
    left: 10px;
    width: 160px;
    height: 120px;
    background: #333333;
  }
  #remote_video {
    position: absolute;
    top: 0px;
    left: 0px;
    width: 1024px;
    height: 768px;
    background: #999999;
  }
</style>
```

Now, we are ready to set up the HTML body content of the page that binds the CSS and JavaScript together into a working user interface. This example application contains only the minimum content needed to demonstrate a working video call application. From this, you should be able to add your own custom content to adapt this to your needs quickly and easily.

```
<body onload="start()">
  <div id="loading_state">
    loading...
  </div>
  <div id="open_call_state">
    <video id="remote_video"></video>
    <video id="local_video"></video>
  </div>
</body>
```

You now have a web page-based user interface and application that can connect two browsers using WebRTC to set up a peer-to-peer video call. From here, you may like to extend this code to add extra error handling, make the WebSocket connection automatically reconnect if it gets disconnected, and also customize the HTML and CSS.

Now that we have set up the browser side of the application, let's move on to see how the signaling server side of this application works.

Setting up a signaling server

In order to provide the web and WebSocket server functionality, we will create a basic Node.js application. You could implement this functionality using any server and programming language of your choice. And you could separate the web component and the WebSocket component into different code bases too. However, for this example, we have integrated them into a single simple JavaScript application to keep it similar to the previous browser side code examples.

This server application really is very simple, is less than 100 lines long, and contains five basic steps:

1. First, we load in some useful libraries that make it easier to implement this application. The most important one is the `websocket` library. If you don't already have that installed in your Node.js implementation, then you should be able to easily install that using `npm`, the node package manager. From the command line, this can be as easy as typing `npm install websocket`.

2. We then define a set of general variables that will be used throughout the application.

3. Next, we set up and define the basic web server behavior for this application.

4. We then set up and define the more detailed WebSocket server functionality that provides the heart of this signaling server application.

5. Finally, we set up some basic utility functions that are used through the application:

```
// useful libs
// general variables
// web server functions
// web socket functions
// utility functions
```

Now, let's walk through each of these five parts of this script in more detail. The first is the useful libs section:

```
// useful libs
```

Within the useful libs section, we start by loading in the "http" package and assigning this to the http variable. This package provides basic web server functionality.

```
var http = require("http");
```

Then, we load in the "fs" package and assign this to the fs variable. This package provides access to the local filesystem on the server so we can read and write files as needed.

```
var fs = require("fs");
```

Then, we load in the websocket package and assign this to the websocket_server variable. This package provides all the functionality we need to setup and configure a WebSocket server.

```
var websocket = require("websocket").server;
```

Now, we can move onto the general variables section:

```
// general variables
```

First, we define a variable that describes on which port our server application will listen. Here, we have picked an arbitrary value for this port. In a production system, this would commonly be 80, which is the standard HTTP port. However, on Unix-like systems, if the application is not running with superuser or root privileges, then it can only use ports above 1000.

```
var port = 1234;
```

Next, we define a simple array that will be used to store a list of the browsers that have open WebSocket connections to this server:

```
var webrtc_clients = [];
```

Then, we define a simple object that will be used to store an indexed list of the different discussions or calls that are currently being managed by this signaling server. The keys that are used to index into this object are call_tokens, set up for each caller.

```
var webrtc_discussions = {};
```

Now, we move onto the web server section of this script:

```
// web server functions
```

First, we use the `http` variable defined just now to call the `createServer()` function to instantiate a running web server and we store a reference to this in the `http_server` variable. This web server provides one single function. It simply returns our HTML page to any browser that sends it a request. In this simple example, we don't care what the request is, but you could easily customize this to handle a wider range of options here.

```
var http_server = http.createServer(function(request, response) {
   response.write(page);
   response.end();
});
```

Then, we bind this `http_server` variable to our chosen port using the `.listen()` function. We also define an anonymous function here that is executed when this server starts.

```
http_server.listen(port, function() {
   log_comment("server listening (port "+port+")");
});
```

Then, we set up our HTML page content that is returned as the response. First, we define a global page variable that is used in the anonymous function passed to the `http.createServer()` call. Then, we use the `fs.readFile()` function to get the contents of our `basic_video_call.html`:

```
var page = undefined;
fs.readFile("basic_video_call.html", function(error, data) {
   if (error) {
     log_error(error);
   } else {
     page = data;
   }
});
```

Next, we move on to the WebSocket section of this script:

```
// web socket functions
```

First we use the `websocket` variable as a constructor and assign this new object to the `websocket_server` variable. We also pass a configuration object to this constructor that tells it to use the `http_server` variable as its `httpServer`:

```
var websocket_server = new websocket({
   httpServer: http_server
});
```

Then, we set up the main function that handles all new requests to this WebSocket server:

```
websocket_server.on("request", function(request) {
  log_comment("new request ("+request.origin+")");
```

By default, we accept all new requests and assign each to a `connection` variable. In a production system, you may want to extend this functionality to add some form of authentication and/or authorization for new connections.

```
var connection = request.accept(null, request.origin);
log_comment("new connection ("+connection.remoteAddress+")");
```

Then, we push this new connection onto the `webrtc_clients` array so that it is added to the list of browsers connected to our server. And, we also use its position in this list to identify this connection easily and store this in the `.id` property of the connection object itself:

```
webrtc_clients.push(connection);
connection.id = webrtc_clients.length-1;
```

Now we are ready to set up the heart of the signaling functionality by defining a function that handles all new messages sent from the connected WebSocket clients:

```
connection.on("message", function(message) {
```

First, we filter out and only handle `utf8`-based messages. You could also extend this to handle binary messages if needed.

```
if (message.type === "utf8") {
  log_comment("got message "+message.utf8Data);
```

Then, we set up a variable that contains the actual signal sent in the message. We try to parse this using the `JSON.parse()` method and wrap this in a `try/catch` block to make sure that non-JSON or invalid JSON messages don't crash this script. In this simple example, we don't do anything at all with errors here, but in your application, you will likely want to extend this to handle all types of error states more elegantly.

```
var signal = undefined;
try { signal = JSON.parse(message.utf8Data); } catch(e) { };
```

Then if the JSON signal was parsed successfully, we use its `.type` property to work out what we should do with it. In this simple example application, we have three key scenarios:

1. If `.type` is `join` and the signal also includes a `.token` property, then we add this connection to the `webrt_discussions` object using the token as the key.

2. Otherwise, if `.type` is anything else and `.token` is defined, then we simply send this message to any other connections that have joined that discussion. You'll also note here that we check to make sure that we don't replay the signal back to the connection that sent this signal to us.

3. In any other case, we simply treat this type of signal as invalid.

Here is the code that handles these three scenarios:

```
if (signal) {
  if (signal.type === "join" && signal.token !== undefined) {
    try {
      if (webrtc_discussions[signal.token] === undefined) {
        webrtc_discussions[signal.token] = {};
      }
    } catch(e) { };
    try {
      webrtc_discussions[signal.token][connection.id] =
        true;
    } catch(e) { };
  } else if (signal.token !== undefined) {
    try {
      Object.keys(webrtc_discussions[signal.token]).
        forEach(function(id) {
        if (id != connection.id) {
          webrtc_clients[id].send(message.utf8Data,
            logg_error);
        }
      });
    } catch(e) { };
  } else {
    log_comment("invalid signal: "+message.utf8Data);
  }
  } else {
    log_comment("invalid signal: "+message.utf8Data);
  }
  }
});
```

Then, we set up a function to handle when connections are closed. Here, we simply walk through the list of all discussions and check to see if this connection has joined them and remove them if necessary. You could make this process more scalable by adding a list of discussions joined to each connection object. This would save you having to walk the full list of all discussions.

```
connection.on("close", function(connection) {
  log_comment("connection
    closed ("+connection.remoteAddress+")");
```

```
    Object.keys(webrtc_discussions).forEach(function(token) {
      Object.keys(webrtc_discussions[token]).forEach(function(id) {
        if (id === connection.id) {
          delete webrtc_discussions[token][id];
        }
      });
    });
  });
});
```

And finally, we can move onto the `utility functions` section of this script:

```
// utility functions
```

First, we have a general `log_error` function which simply prints errors to the console. You may want to extend this to handle errors more elegantly and where relevant, send notifications back to any connections that have been impacted.

```
function log_error(error) {
  if (error !== "Connection closed" && error !== undefined) {
    log_comment("ERROR: "+error);
  }
}
```

Finally, we have a simple `log_comment` function that takes a comment string and prepends it with a timestamp and then writes this to the console:

```
function log_comment(comment) {
  console.log((new Date())+" "+comment);
}
```

Now you have a fully working `webrtc_signaling_server.js` script that supports both web and WebSocket connections. A browser can connect to it to load the `basic_video_call.html` web page which will then automatically set up a WebSocket connection too.

Creating an offer in the caller's browser

As the caller, you are the person initiating the call. You visit the web page first and get `call_token` that you then share with the person to which you want to connect. But then your browser has to wait until the callee connects.

Once they do connect, their browser sends a signal to the signaling server letting it know that they have arrived, and this signal is then sent to your browser. Once your browser receives this `callee_arrived` signal, you can then initiate the JSEP offer/answer process by calling `peer_connection.createOffer()`:

```
// handle signals as a caller
function caller_signal_handler(event) {
  var signal = JSON.parse(event.data);
  if (signal.type === "callee_arrived") {
    peer_connection.createOffer(
      new_description_created,
      log_error
    );
  } else …
}
```

If the offer is created successfully, then the resulting description is passed to the `new_description_created()` function. This calls `peer_connection.setLocalDescription()` to set this as the local description and then serializes this description, and sends it to the signaling server as a `new_description` signal that is then forwarded on to the remote browser:

```
// handler to process new descriptions
function new_description_created(description) {
  peer_connection.setLocalDescription(
    description,
    function () {
      signaling_server.send(
        JSON.stringify({
          call_token:call_token,
          type:"new_description",
          sdp:description
        })
      );
    },
    log_error
  );
}
```

Creating an answer in the callee's browser

Once you have connected to the web page as a callee, and the caller's browser has initiated the JSEP offer/answer process, you will receive a new_description signal. We then call peer_connect.setRemoteDescription() to set this as the remote description, and if this description is really an offer, then we call peer_connection. createAnswer() to send back a response. Just like in the code snippet for the caller, we use the new_description_created() function to set this answer as our local description, and then serialize it into a new_description signal that is then sent back to the caller:

```
// handle signals as a callee
function callee_signal_handler(event) {
  ...
    } else if (signal.type === "new_description") {
      peer_connection.setRemoteDescription(
        new rtc_session_description(signal.sdp),
        function () {
          if (peer_connection.remoteDescription.type == "offer") {
            peer_connection.createAnswer(new_description_created, log_
error);
          }
        },
        log_error
      );
    } else ...
}
```

Previewing the local video streams

To preview the local video streams, we implement the setup_video() function. This requests access to the local camera's video stream using the getUserMedia call.

If this stream is set up successfully, then it is displayed on the local browser page in the <video> media element with the local_video ID using the connect_stream_ to_src() function defined in webrtc_polyfill.js.

If this local stream is not set up successfully, then the error is logged so the user can be notified.

```
// setup stream from the local camera
function setup_video() {
  get_user_media(
```

```
    {
      "audio": true, // request access to local microphone
      "video": true  // request access to local camera
    },
    function (local_stream) { // success callback
      // preview the local camera & microphone stream
      connect_stream_to_src(
        local_stream,
        document.getElemntById("local_video")
      );
      ...
    },
    log_error // error callback
  );
}
```

It is important that this function is called and the streams are added to the peer connection object before any other code attempts to create an offer or an answer.

Establishing peer-to-peer streams

When the setup_video() function is called, and the stream is set up successfully, then it is added to peer_connection using the peer_connection. addStream(local_stream) call. This is then ready to be sent to the remote peer automatically once the full RTCPeerConnection is set up successfully.

```
// setup stream from the local camera
function setup_video() {
  get_user_media(
    {
      "audio": true, // request access to local microphone
      "video": true  // request access to local camera
    },
    function (local_stream) { // success callback
      ...
      // add local stream to peer_connection ready to be sent to the
remote peer
      peer_connection.addStream(local_stream);
    },
    log_error // error callback
  );
}
```

Once the stream from the remote peer is received, then the `peer_connection.onaddstream` handler is called. This uses the `connect_stream_to_src()` method defined in the `webrtc_polyfill.js` code to display the stream in the `<video>` media element with the `remote_video` ID. If your user interface shows the user a placeholder user interface until the remote stream is received, then this is where you will also want to add code to update this state.

```
// display remote video streams when they arrive
peer_connection.onaddstream = function (event) {
    // hide placeholder and show remote video
    connect_stream_to_src(
        event.stream,
        document.getElementById("remote_video")
    );
};
```

Stream processing options

Once you have set up any video stream from either a local or remote source to display within a `<video>` element on your page, you can then access this data to process it in any number of ways. You can create filters to change colors, create **chromakey** effects, or do facial/object recognition, just to name a few.

Here's a brief overview of how you access the data within these streams to set up this type of processing:

1. Set up a `<canvas>` element in the DOM.
   - declaratively then via `getElementById` or similar
   - `createElement("canvas")`, then `appendChild()`

2. Get a 2D drawing context for `<canvas>`.
   ```
   canvas_context = canvas.getContext('2d');
   ```

3. Draw the `<video>` frames onto `<canvas>`.
   ```
   canvas_context.drawImage(video, top, left, width, height);
   ```

4. Get the RGBA Uint8ClampedArray of the pixels.
   ```
   context.getImageData(top, left, width, height).data;
   ```

5. Loop through the typed array to process pixel rows and columns.
   ```
   for (...) { for (...) { … } … }
   ```

6. Render results.

   ◦ using HTML/JS/CSS

   ◦ using another `<canvas>` and `drawImage()`

   ◦ using WebGL

   ◦ a combination of all

> Here are some links to some useful examples to help you get started.
> Chromakey/greenscreen:
>
> `https://developer.mozilla.org/en-US/docs/HTML/`
> `Manipulating_video_using_canvas`
>
> Exploding video:
>
> `http://shinydemos.com/explode/`
>
> Face detection:
>
> `https://github.com/neave/face-detection`
>
> Head tracking:
>
> `https://github.com/auduno/headtrackr`
>
> Image processing pipeline:
>
> `https://github.com/buildar/getting_started_with_`
> `webrtc/blob/master/image_processing_pipeline.html`

Extending this example into a Chatroulette app

Now that you have a working application that connects two users in a peer-to-peer video call, you can easily extend this in a number of ways. One option is to change the setup and signaling flow so that callees are connected to random callers just like the video Chatroulette applications that have sprung up all across the Internet. Have a look at this Google search, `https://www.google.com/` `search?q=video+chat+roulette`.

To implement this type of functionality, you only need to make two simple changes.

First, each browser that connects to the web page can randomly be allocated as either a caller or a callee, removing the need for the caller to send a link with `call_token` to the callee. In this new application, users just visit the web page and are automatically entered into either the caller or callee scenario.

Second, update the signaling server so that when a callee joins, the signaling server loops through the `webrtc_discussions` object looking for callers who are not currently connected to anyone else. The signaling server would then return `call_token` for that discussion and the signaling flow works like normal after that.

This shows you just how easy it is to extend this basic example application to create all sorts of new applications using WebRTC.

Summary

You should now have a clear understanding of how to create a fully working application that connects two users in a WebRTC-based peer-to-peer video call. You should be able to utilize the MediaStream and RTCPeerConnection APIs in real world scenarios and understand how these different components work together in a living application.

You should be able to set up a web server that handles the initial process of connecting two users and set up a signaling server that manages the setup of the video call. You should understand in detail how the caller's browser initiates the JSEP offer and how the callee's browser responds with an answer. You should have a clear knowledge of how the local and remote video streams are connected to and displayed in the web page, how these streams can be processed to create filters and other special effects, and how this example application can easily be extended.

In the next chapters, we will explore how this application can be simplified down to just an audio only call or extended with text-based chat and file sharing.

And then we will explore two real-world application scenarios based upon e-learning and team communication.

Creating an Audio Only Call

4

This chapter shows you how to turn on the video chat application, which we had developed in the previous chapter into an audio only call application. After reading this chapter you will have a clear understanding of:

- Setting up an HTML user interface for audio only calls
- Handling audio only signaling
- The types of audio stream processing available

Setting up a simple WebRTC audio only call

In the previous chapter, we had developed an application that implemented the most common WebRTC example of setting up a video call between two browsers. But sometimes, you may not have enough bandwidth to support video streaming, the browsers may not have cameras connected, or the users may just prefer to simply participate in a voice call instead. Here, we will show how easy it is to adapt the existing application we have developed to turn it into an audio only application.

The HTML user interface for audio only calls

First, let's look at how the HTML-based web page will need to be modified. As before, we start with a standard HTML5 web page that includes a DOCTYPE definition, a document head, and a document body.

```
<!DOCTYPE html>
<html>
<head>
...
</head>
<body>
...
</body>
</html>
```

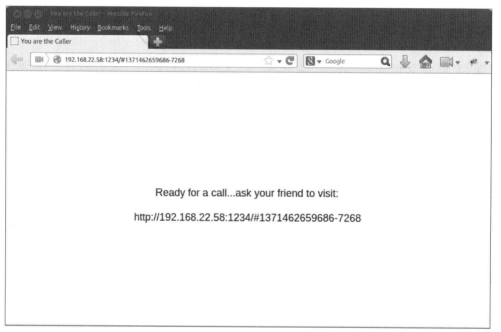

The Caller interface ready for another browser to join the call

And again, the first element inside the document head is a pair of <script> tags that include the webrtc_polyfill.js code inline.

This is followed by the code that defines the `basic_audio_call.js` browser side logic, included inline within a pair of `<script></script>` tags. This code will only require minor modifications to the one we developed in the previous chapter, and we'll discuss all this in more detail.

Then, the simple CSS-based styles are defined within a pair of `<style></style>` tags, as before.

And finally, the HTML body content of the page is defined to bind the CSS and JavaScript together into a working user interface.

```
<body onload="start()">
  <div id="loading_state">
    loading...
  </div>
  <div id="open_call_state">
    <audio id="remote_audio"></audio>
  </div>
</body>
```

Here you will notice that only two small changes have been made to the HTML body content:

- The first `<video>` element has been changed to an `<audio>` media element, and its ID has been updated to `remote_audio`.

- The second `<video>` element that was used to preview the local camera stream has been removed. In an audio only call, it doesn't make sense to play back the stream from the local microphone, as this will cause feedback.

You will probably want to extend this user interface to provide other options such as the ability to hang up the call, and so on. In fact, without the `<video>` elements, the user interface is effectively empty. But these two HTML modifications are the simplest changes required for this example.

Then, we need to update the function that requests access to the local microphone's audio stream using the `getUserMedia` call and rename this to `setup_audio()`. In the video call application, if this stream is set up successfully, it is displayed on the local browser's page in a `<video>` element. However, since we want to avoid the screech of audio feedback from the local microphone, we only need to add this stream to the `peer_connection` object, so that it can be sent to the remote peer's browser. And as usual, if this local stream is not set up successfully, the error is logged so the user can be notified.

```
// setup stream from the local microphone
function setup_audio() {
    get_user_media(
```

```
        {
          "audio": true, // request access to local microphone
          "video": false  // don't request access to local camera
        },
        function (local_stream) { // success callback
          ...
        },
        log_error // error callback
      );
  }
```

Now, we are ready to make the final three updates to the JavaScript:

- Change the `peer_connection.onaddstream` handler to use `document.getElementById("remote_audio")` instead of `document.getElementById("remote_video")`

- Change the `caller_signal_handler()` function so the `callee_arrived` flow ends by calling `setup_audio()` instead of `setup_video()`

- Change the `callee_signal_handler()` function so the `new_description` flow ends by calling `setup_audio()` instead of `setup_video()`

The web browser side of this new audio only call application is now complete.

Adding an audio only flow to the signaling server

The WebSocket-based signaling server we developed in `node.js` was designed in an abstract way, so that it only used `call_token` to route signals from one user to another. Other than that, it doesn't have any specific dependencies upon the contents or type of signaling messages at all. This means that no updates to the signaling server are required to adapt it to support audio only calls.

The only change required is to update the name of the source HTML file it reads in using the `fs` package. Just change this to `basic_audio_call.html` to match our new HTML user interface:

```
    fs.readFile("basic_audio_call.html", function(error, data) {
```

Once you have made this simple change, just restart the signaling server; for example, by typing `node webrtc_signal_server.js` on the command line, and then you are ready to start making your audio only call.

Audio stream processing options

As with video streams, once you have set up any audio streams from either a local or remote source to an `<audio>` media element, you can then start to explore processing the binary data using JavaScript. The evolving Web Audio API is designed to bring rich audio processing to the web and allows you to add filters and effects, visualize your audio streams, and much more. The latest specification of the Web Audio API is available at `http://www.w3.org/TR/webaudio/`, you can find some great example applications by *Chris Wilson* at `http://webaudiodemos.appspot.com/`.

Summary

You should now have a clear understanding of how easy it is to adapt our existing video call application to support audio only calls. You should be able to update the HTML user interface to adapt from video to audio. And you should now understand how the cleanly abstracted design of the signaling server requires no real updates to support this new application scenario.

You should also have all the information you need to start exploring how these audio streams can be processed to create filters and other special effects.

In the next chapters, we will explore how this application can be extended with text based chat and file sharing.

And then, we will explore two real-world application scenarios based on e-learning and team communication.

5
Adding Text-based Chat

This chapter shows you how to extend the video chat application we developed in *Chapter 2, A More Technical Introduction to Web-based Real-Time Communication*, to add support for text-based chat between the two users. After reading this chapter, you will have a clear understanding of:

- Extending the existing HTML to support text-based chat
- Adding additional JavaScript to enable chatting
- Handling text-based chat in the signaling server
- Other chat-based message processing ideas and options

Adding text-based chat to our video chat app

In the previous chapter, we explored how you could simplify your video chat application for when you want to offer "audio only" calls. Now, let's see how easy it is to extend our original video chat application so that the two users can also chat by typing messages and they can share web links and notes, as they interact through the video interface.

The HTML user interface for text-based chat

First, let's look at how the HTML-based web page will need to be modified. As usual, we start with a standard HTML5 web page that includes a DOCTYPE definition, a document head, and a document body.

```
<!DOCTYPE html>
<html>
<head>
...
</head>
<body>
...
</body>
</html>
```

And again, the first element inside the document head is a pair of <script> tags that includes the webrtc_polyfill.js script.

As before, this is followed by the video_call_with_chat.js code that defines the browser side logic included inline within a pair of <script></script> tags. This code only differs slightly from the original basic_video_call.js code, and we'll walk through this in detail now.

Next, our simple CSS-based styles are defined within a pair of <style></style> tags as usual with style definitions for chat, messages, and message_input ID's.

Then as usual, the HTML body content of the page is defined to bind the CSS and JavaScript together into a working user interface.

```
<body onload="start()">
  <div id="loading_state">
    loading...
  </div>
  <div id="open_call_state">
    <video id="remote_video"></video>
    <video id="local_video"></video>
    <div id="chat">
      <div id="messages"></div>
      <input type="text"
        id="message_input"
        value="Type here then hit enter..."></input>
    </div>
  </div>
</body>
```

Here you will notice that three changes have been made to the HTML `body` content:

1. We have added a general `chat` div container within which the entire text-based chat user interface is wrapped.

2. Then we have added a `messages` div into which we will add all new messages as lines of text as they either arrive from the signaling server, or are entered by the local user.

3. Finally, we have added a `message_input` text input field so you can type your messages to send to the person on the other end of your call.

A live video call with the text-based chat panel added on the right

You easily extend this user interface to add different colors to the names that prefix each message, add timestamps, allow users to set their nickname, and so on. But these three HTML modifications are the simplest changes required for this example.

Adding JavaScript functions to enable chatting

Next, we need to add a few simple functions that will handle the chat messages received from the signaling server and that will enable the local users to send their own messages.

At the end of the existing `start()` function, we add two calls that define some basic functionality for the `message_input` bar.

The first step is to add an `onkeydown` event handler that checks each new character entered into the `message_input` bar, and if the latest one is a return, then it takes the full value of the message and sends it to the signaling server as a `new_chat_message`.

```
document.getElementById("message_input").onkeydown =
    send_chat_message;
```

The second step is to add a simple `onfocus` event handler that clears the `message_input` bar so that you can start typing a new message. By default, we start with a simple hint that says `Type here then hit enter...` and we need to clear this as soon as you bring focus to the `message_input` bar.

```
document.getElementById("message_input").onfocus =
    function() { this.value = ""; }
```

Next, we add an extra `else if ()` block to both the `caller_signal_handler()` and `callee_signal_handler()` functions:

```
} else if (signal.type === "new_chat_message") {
    add_chat_message(signal);
} ...
```

This detects new inbound signals sent from the signaling server where the type is `new_chat_message`, and then directs them to the `add_chat_message()` function.

This then takes these new messages and adds them to the `messages` div wrapper within the chat user interface. This function is the perfect place to add extra functionality, based on which user the message comes from or other types of context.

```
function add_chat_message(signal) {
  var messages = document.getElementById("messages");
  var user = signal.user || "them";
  messages.innerHTML =
    user+": "+signal.message+"<br/>\n"+messages.innerHTML;
}
```

The video chat application we developed in *Chapter 2, A More Technical Introduction to Web-based Real-Time Communication*, now has all the functionality it needs to support text-based chat.

Handling text-based chat signals on the server

As in the audio call only example, here again we can see that the abstract design of the WebSocket-based signaling server we developed requires no updates to support text-based chat.

The only change required is to update the name of the source HTML file it reads in using the `fs` package to `video_call_with_chat.html` to match our new HTML user interface:

```
fs.readFile("video_call_with_chat.html", function(error, data) {
```

Just make this change, and then restart the signaling server, and you are ready to start chatting using text alongside your video call.

Other text message processing options

Now that you can easily type text messages to send to the other browser, you can add all kinds of other functionality. If you look at common instant messaging systems such as **Internet Relay Chat (IRC)**, Skype, or any of the systems based on **Extensible Messaging and Presence Protocol(XMPP)**, you'll see that they support emoticons (for example, smileys such as ;)) that are automatically converted into image-based icons.

Many of these systems also support special command strings that allow you to access predefined functionality. Because this chat application is simply HTML, CSS, and JavaScript-based code you have developed, you can easily add custom functions to do things, such as play sounds, update the user interface, or anything else you can imagine. Then, simply define some specific symbolic strings (for example, like #hashtags in Twitter) that you can easily detect and use to trigger these functions.

This text-based chat solution is based on sending messages through the WebSocket API via the signaling server. Another option that has a very similar interface is the RTCDataChannel API. This is not as stable or as widely supported as WebSocket, or the RTCPeerConnection and MediaStream APIs, but it does have some great advantages that we'll explore in the next chapter.

Summary

You should now have a clear understanding of how easy it is to adapt our initial video call application to support text-based chat. You should be able to update the HTML user interface to add a simple chat panel. And you should now appreciate even more how the cleanly abstracted design of the signaling server allows us to easily support new application scenarios.

You should also have all the information you need to start exploring other text message processing options and ideas.

In the next chapters, we will explore how this application can be extended to also support file sharing.

And then, we will explore two real-world application scenarios based upon e-learning and team communication.

6

Adding File Sharing

This chapter shows you how to extend the video chat application we developed in the second and fourth chapters to add support for file sharing between the two users. After reading this chapter, you will have a clear understanding of:

- Extending the existing HTML for supporting file sharing
- Adding JavaScript for enabling file sharing
- Adding files through the standard file selector user interface
- Enabling users to drag-and-drop files into the browser window
- Adding JavaScript for transferring files over the WebSocket connection
- Extending the signaling server for supporting file transfer
- Sending thumbnails before sending the whole file
- Providing progress updates during the transfer
- Using RTCDataChannel connections between two users
- Adding JavaScript for transferring files over the RTCDataChannel connection
- Other file sharing related ideas and options

Adding file sharing to our video chat app

In the previous chapter, we explored how we could extend our video chat application to add text based chat. Now, let's see how we can add a whole new layer to this video chat application that enables the two users to also share files by selecting them through a file selector or dragging them into the browser window.

The HTML user interface for file sharing

First, let's look at how the HTML-based web page needs to be modified. As usual, we start with a standard HTML5 web page that includes a DOCTYPE definition, a document head, and a document body:

```
<!DOCTYPE html>
<html>
<head>
...
</head>
<body>
...
</body>
</html>
```

And again the first element inside the document head is a pair of `<script></script>` tags that includes the `webrtc_polyfill.js` script.

As before, this is followed by the `video_call_with_chat_and_file_sharing.js` code that defines the browser side logic included inline within a pair of `<script></script>` tags. This code differs slightly from the original `basic_video_call_with_chat.js` code, and we'll walk through this in detail.

Next, our simple CSS-based styles are defined within a pair of `<style></style>` tags, as usual with style definitions for `file_sharing`, `file_input`, `file_add`, `file_list`, `file_img_src`, and `file_thumbnail_canvas` id's added along with definitions for `file`, `file_img`, and `file_progress` classes.

Then, as usual, the HTML body content of the page is defined to bind the CSS and JavaScript together into a working user interface, as shown in the following code:

```
<body onload="start()">
  <div id="loading_state">
    loading...
  </div>
  <div id="open_call_state">
    <video id="remote_video"></video>
    <video id="local_video"></video>
    <div id="chat">
      <div id="messages"></div>
      <input type="text"
        id="message_input"
        value="Type here then hit enter..."></input>
```

```
        </div>
        <div id="file_sharing">
          <input type="file" id="file_input"></input>
          <div id="file_add">
            <img src="images/share_new_file.png" />
          </div>
          <div id="file_list">
          </div>
          <img id="file_img_src" />
          <canvas id="file_thumbnail_canvas"></canvas>
        </div>
      </div>
    </body>
```

Here you will notice that we have added a `file_sharing` div that contains five new elements:

- First, we have added a `file_input` element that allows the browser to access the file system.

- Next, we have added a `file_add` div that contains a single image that acts as the **Share a new file** button.

- Then, we have added a `file_list` div that will contain the list of new files as they are added to the user interface.

- Next, we have a hidden `file_img_src` image element that is used in the process of creating the thumbnail preview of the shared files. This process will be described in detail in a short while.

- Finally, we have a hidden `file_thumbnail_canvas` element that is also used in the process of creating the thumbnail previews.

These additions will provide an intuitive user interface that lets the user click on a button to share a file or simply drag the file into the browser window. A preview of the file will be displayed in a list on the left under the local camera preview. And the file preview list automatically shows the progress of the file transfer, and once fully transferred, it allows you to view the full file by simply clicking on the thumbnail.

This demonstration application has focused on the more complex process of sharing image files. From here, you should be able to extend this to support sharing documents and other file types easily, replacing the image thumbnails with your own file icons.

Adding JavaScript for enabling file sharing

First, we add a new global variable that is used to hold all the data that defines the list of files that have been shared.

```
var file_store = []; // shared file storage
```

Then, at the end of the `start()` function, we add an `if/else` block, which detects if our browser supports all of the capabilities required to enable file sharing.

```
// setup file sharing
if (!(window.File
      && window.FileReader
      && window.FileList
      && window.Blob)) {
  document.getElementById("file_sharing").style.display =
"none";
  alert("This browser does not support File Sharing");
} else {
  document.getElementById("file_add").onclick =
    click_file_input;
  document.getElementById("file_input").addEventListener("change",
      file_input, false);
  document.getElementById("open_call_state").addEventListener("drago
ver", drag_over, false);
  document.getElementById("open_call_state").
addEventListener("drop", file_input, false);
}
```

If it doesn't support the required capabilities, we hide the file sharing user interface and notify the user.

Otherwise, we bind four handlers to elements within the page to activate the file sharing functionality:

- A `file_add onclick` handler that enables manual file selection

- A `file_input change` event handler that detects when the file input element has received one or more new files

- A `dragover` event handler for the whole user interface that detects when something has been dragged over the user interface

- A `drop` event handler for the whole user interface that detects when something has been dropped onto the user interface

Adding files using the <input> element

The first thing you will notice when you use this version of the application is that there is now a **Share a new file** button sitting underneath the local video preview window at the top left-hand corner of the user interface. As you saw previously, this button is bound to the `click_file_input()` function using an `onclick` event handler. This is a very simple function that triggers the `click` event on the `file_input` element itself.

```
// initiate manual file selection
function click_file_input(event) {
    document.getElementById('file_input').click();
}
```

Doing so allows us to use an image button and hide the default `file_input` element, so that we can easily customize the design of the user interface as per our choice and not just limited by the design constraints of the input element.

This then prompts the browser to present the user with the native file selection user interface. Once the user has selected the file of his/her choice, then the `file_input` `change` event handler is fired, which calls the `file_input()` function.

```
// handle manual file selection or drop event
function file_input(event) {
  ...
    files = event.target.files;
  ...
  if (files.length > 1) {
    alert("Please only select one file at a time");
  } else if (!files[0].type.match('image.*')) {
    alert("This demo only supports sharing image files");
  } else if (files.length == 1) {
    ...
  }
}
```

Because the `change` event on the `file_input` element triggered this call, the event object should contain a target property, which is a reference to the input itself. This will then contain a files property that is a collection of the files selected by the user.

For this application, we will only handle the case where one file is selected at a time. You can easily extend this for multiple files support. You will also notice that we have limited the selection to image files only. The following code example handles the creation of a small thumbnail from the image and sending that before slicing up and sending the entire large file. You can also extend this code to support other file types that utilize your own file icons, and so on.

So, now that we have asserted that only one single image file has been selected, we can move onto the process of handling this file:

```
          var kb = (files[0].size/1024).toFixed(1);
    var new_message = "Sending file...<br><strong>"+
                                      files[0].name+"</strong>
("+kb+"KB)";
    signaling_server.send(
      JSON.stringify({
        token:call_token,
        type: "new_chat_message",
        message: new_message
      })
    );
    add_chat_message({ user: "you", message: new_message });
```

First, we build a message that describes this new file. We create a variable named kb that determines the size of this file in kilobytes. Then, we combine this along with the file's name into the message. We then send this new_message to the other user to let them know that we are about to start sending this file. And, we also add this message to our local chat messages list so we know what is happening. All of this is done using the existing text chat structure we added to this application in *Chapter 4, Creating an Audio Only Call.*

Next, we inject the HTML code that displays this file into our list of shared files. We do this using the get_file_div() function that returns the HTML template for this code:

```
    document.getElementById("file_list").innerHTML =
        get_file_div(file_store.length)+
            document.getElementById("file_list").innerHTML;
```

Next, we read the selected file from the filesystem and convert it into a base64 data URL, as shown in the following code:

```
    var reader = new FileReader();
    reader.onload = (function(file, id) {
      return function(event) {
        send_file(file.name, id, event.target.result);
      }
    })(files[0], file_store.length);
    reader.readAsDataURL(files[0]);
```

You will notice that we have first set up an `onload` handler and then called the `readAsDataURL()` function. This is important, because loading the file can take some time and this ensures that the `send_file()` function isn't called until the file is fully loaded. The `send_file()` function then creates a thumbnail and sends that first, followed by the full file itself. We will walk through this process in more detail later.

In this application, we use the base64 data URL file format for interacting with canvas elements, within file transfers, and for rendering into a window to display the entire file. However, in many cases you may find it is more efficient to use binary data in typed arrays, and this is an area that I would' strongly encourage you to explore further. The html5rocks website provides an excellent introduction to typed arrays at `http://www.html5rocks.com/en/tutorials/webgl/typed_arrays/`.

Adding support for drag-and-drop

While it's easy for a user to click on the **Share a new file** button, it is also convenient to allow them to simply drag a file into the browser window. Previously we added two event handlers that deal with the `dragover` and `drop` events and we bound this to `open_call_state` which effectively fills the entire browser viewport. This means that you can now drag a file onto any part of the browser window to initiate the file sharing transfer.

First, we create the `drag_over()` function that simply prevents the browser from leaving our web page and loading the file that was dragged into it, which is the default browser behavior.

```
// prevent window from reloading when file dragged into it
function drag_over(event) {
  event.stopPropagation();
  event.preventDefault();
}
```

Then, within the `file_input()` function, we have some additional lines of code:

```
function file_input(event) {
  event.stopPropagation();
  event.preventDefault();
  var files = undefined;
  if (event.dataTransfer.files !== undefined) {
    files = event.dataTransfer.files;
  } else if (event.target.files !== undefined) {
    files = event.target.files;
  }
  ...
}
```

First, we call `event.stopPropagation` and `event.preventDefault()` to ensure that the default browser behavior doesn't interfere with how we want our user interface to behave.

Then, we check if the event object contains a `dataTransfer` property, which contains a list of files. If yes, we use that; otherwise, we fall back to the `event.target.files` approach because we can then assume that the `file_input()` function was called by the manual file selection instead.

And that's all we need to do to enable drag-and-drop based file sharing. The rest of the file sharing functionality works the same, irrespective of whether the shared file is selected manually or dragged into the browser window.

Adding JavaScript for transferring files via WebSockets

We will discuss the RTCDataChannel-based file sharing, but first let's look at how we can implement this using WebSockets. The `file_input()` function described previously calls the following `send_file()` function.

```
// send selected file
function send_file(name, file_id, data) {
  ...
  var img = document.getElementById("file_img_src");
  img.onload = function() {
    ...
    send_file_parts("file", file_id, data);
  }
  img.src = data;
}
```

First, we select the `file_img_src` element that we will use for loading the file data. Then, we set up an `onload` handler, and at the end of this, we call `send_file_parts()`. This will slice the file data into chunks and send each of them to the other server once the image has fully loaded. Then, we start the whole process by assigning the data to `image.src`.

Now, let's look at the `send_file_parts()` function:

```
// break file into parts and send each of them separately
function send_file_parts(type, id, data) {
  var message_type = "new_file_part";
  ...
  var slice_size = 1024;
```

```
    var parts = data.length/slice_size;
    if (parts % 1 > 0) {
      parts = Math.round(parts)+1;
    }
    for (var i = 0; i < parts; i++) {
      var from = i*slice_size;
      var to = from+slice_size;
      var data_slice = data.slice(from, to);
      store_file_part(type, id, i, parts, data_slice);
      signaling_server.send(
        JSON.stringify({
          token:call_token,
          type: message_type,
          id: id,
          part: i,
          length: parts,
          data: data_slice
        })
      );
    }
  }
```

First, we set `message_type` to `new_file_part` and then set the `slice_size` to `1024` characters. Then we work out how many parts we can slice the data into, and then we loop through this process extracting a `data.slice()` each time and send it through `signaling_server`.

Before we send each slice to `signaling_server`, we also store a copy of this in the local `file_store`. And, when we receive a file part from the other browser, we also use the same function to store these parts in the local `file_store`.

```
// store individual file parts in the local file store
function store_file_part(type, id, part, length, data) {
  if (file_store[id] === undefined) {
    file_store[id] = {};
  }
  if (file_store[id][type] === undefined) {
    file_store[id][type] = {
      parts: []
    };
  }
  if (file_store[id][type].length === undefined) {
    file_store[id][type].length = length;
  }
  file_store[id][type].parts[part] = data;
}
```

Within the `start()` function, we also extend the signal handling code for both the caller and the callee to handle the `new_file_part` message type.

```
    } else if (signal.type === "new_file_part") {
      store_file_part("file", signal.id, signal.part, signal.length,
  signal.data);
      update_file_progress(signal.id,
        file_store[signal.id].file.parts.length,
        signal.length);
```

The previous code stores each part as it is received, and then calls the `update_file_progress()` function that we will explore in more detail in a while.

Each file thumbnail also has an `onclick` handler included within the HTML template that is bound to the `display_file()` function:

```
// show the full file
function display_file(event) {
  var match = event.target.id.match("file-img-(.*)");
  var file = file_store[match[1]].file;
  if (file.parts.length < file.length) {
    alert("Please wait - file still transfering");
  } else {
    window.open(file.parts.join(""));
  }
}
```

This function lets users view the full image file in a new window by clicking on the thumbnail image in the shared file list. We also add in a simple check to make sure that the file has finished transferring before we let the user view it.

Handling the file-sharing signals on the server

As in the audio call only and text chat examples, yet again we can see that the abstract design of the WebSocket based signaling server requires almost no updates to support file sharing.

The primary change allows us to handle serving image files from an images/ directory so we can include the **Share a new file** button image and the new file-arriving placeholder image.

```
  // web server functions
var http_server = http.createServer(function(request, response) {
    var matches = undefined;
```

```
if (matches = request.url.match("^/images/(.*)")) {
    var path = process.cwd()+"/images/"+matches[1];
    fs.readFile(path, function(error, data) {
        if (error) {
            log_error(error);
        } else {
            response.end(data);
        }
    });
} else {
    response.end(page);
}
});
```

The only other change required is to update the name of the source HTML file it reads in using the `fs` package to `video_call_with_chat_and_file_sharing.html` to match our new HTML user interface.

```
fs.readFile("video_call_with_chat_and_file_sharing.html",
    function(error, data) {
```

Just make this change, and then restart the signaling server, and you are ready to start sharing files within your video call.

Sending a thumbnail preview before the entire file

In order to create a friendlier and more responsive user interface, we have set up the `send_file` process as a pipeline. First, it creates a thumbnail version of the image that is scaled to fit within the 160px by 120px image area. Then, we slice this thumbnail image and first send it to the other browser so it can be displayed while the full data is being transferred. Then, we transfer the full data:

```
// send selected file
function send_file(name, file_id, data) {
    var default_width = 160;
    var default_height = 120;
    var img = document.getElementById("file_img_src");
```

First, we set up the default width and height for the image area and select the hidden `file_img_src` element that we use in the first step of the thumbnail creation process.

```
img.onload = function() {
    var image_width = this.width;
    var target_width = default_width;
```

```
var image_height = this.height;
var target_height = default_height;
var top = 0;
var left = 0;
```

Then, within the `onload` function, we set up the variables we will use to scale the image to fit within the 160px by 120px image area:

```
if (image_width > image_height) {
  var ratio = target_width/image_width;
  target_height = image_height*ratio;
  top = (default_height-target_height)/2;
} else if (image_height > image_width) {
  var ratio = target_height/image_height;
  target_width = image_width*ratio;
  left = (default_width-target_width)/2;
} else {
  left = (default_width-default_height)/2;
  target_width = target_height;
}
```

We check if the image is wider than its height. If it is, then we work out the ratio of `target_width` to the actual `image_width`. Then we multiply `image_height` by this ratio to get `target_height`. Then we work out the difference between `default_height` and `target_height` and divide the difference by 2 to get the vertical offset.

If the image wasn't wider than its height, we check if it was taller than it is wide and apply a similar process. Otherwise, it is a square image, and we adjust the scaling algorithm appropriately.

Next, we select the hidden `file_thumbnail_canvas` and call `getContext("2d")` to create a drawing context for this canvas, as shown in the following code:

```
var canvas = document.getElementById("file_thumbnail_canvas");
canvas.width = default_width;
canvas.height = default_height;
var cc = canvas.getContext("2d");
cc.clearRect(0,0,default_width,default_height);
cc.drawImage(img, left, top, target_width, target_height);
var thumbnail_data = canvas.toDataURL("image/png");
document.getElementById("file-img-"+file_id).src =
  thumbnail_data;
send_file_parts("thumbnail", file_id, thumbnail_data);
send_file_parts("file", file_id, data);
}
img.src = data;
}
```

We call the `drawImage()` function on this context to render the image scaled down to the size of the thumbnail image that we had calculated. Then, we call `canvas.toDataURL("image/png")` to convert this thumbnail image into a base64 data URL string, as discussed earlier.

We then pass this `thumbnail_data` to the `send_file_parts()` function before we pass the full data object to the `send_file_parts()` function.

We also need to extend the signal handling in the `start()` function for both the caller and the callee to handle the `new_file_thumbnail_part` signal `message_type`.

```
    } else if (signal.type === "new_file_thumbnail_part") {
        store_file_part("thumbnail", signal.id, signal.part,
            signal.length, signal.data);
        if (file_store[signal.id].thumbnail.parts.length ==
            signal.length) {
            document.getElementById("file_list").innerHTML =
                get_file_div(signal.id)+document.getElementById("file_list").
inner
  HTML;
            document.getElementById("file-img-"+signal.id).src =
                file_store[signal.id].thumbnail.parts.join("");
        }
```

This code calls the `store_file_part()` function just as the `new_file_part` signal handler does. And then it checks if this part completes the transfer for this file. If it does, then it injects the file HTML template into the top of `file_list` and assigns all the combined parts into the `file-img-n` element's `.src` property to display the thumbnail image.

Providing progress updates

To help the user understand when a file is still in the process of being transferred, we have added some extra code. When a thumbnail first appears it is set to be semi-transparent, and over the top of it we display a number that shows the percentage of this file that has been transferred. The `update_file_progress()` function that handles this logic is called from the `new_file_part` signal handler for both the caller and the callee, and it uses values included in the `new_file_part` signal.

```
// show the progress of a file transfer
function update_file_progress(id, parts, length) {
  var percentage = Math.round((parts/length)*100);
  if (percentage < 100) {
    document.getElementById("file-progress-"+id).innerHTML =
      percentage+"%";
    document.getElementById("file-img-"+id).style.opacity = 0.25;
```

```
    } else {
      document.getElementById("file-progress-"+id).innerHTML = "";
      document.getElementById("file-img-"+id).style.opacity = 1;
    }
  }
```

First, we take the number of parts transferred so far and the length or total number of parts, and use these variables to work out what percentage has been transferred so far. If this is less than 100, we set the thumbnail's opacity to 0.25 and update the text to show the percentage value. If this is 100, we set the thumbnail's opacity to 1 and set the percentage value to an empty string so it is no longer shown.

Establishing an RTCDataChannel connection

At the time of writing this chapter, the RTCDataChannel implementations are not completely stable and are not inter operable between the different mainstream browsers. However, the RTCDataChannel API has been designed to be almost identical to the WebSocket API when it is being used, so the general code and application logic we have defined previously should be able to be easily migrated to the RTCDataChannel API when it is ready.

The primary difference is that the WebSocket API uses a new `WebSocket()` based constructor, but the RTCDataChannel API uses a `peer_connection.createDataChannel()` based constructor.

However, after the offer/answer flow is completed, the RTCDataChannel event model is almost identical to the WebSocket API.

Transfering files via an RTCDataChannel connection

The model here is the same as interacting with `signaling_server`, except in this case the data is flowing directly to the other peer instead via the WebSocket server.

To send some data you simply call the `data_channel.send()` function just as you call the `signaling_server.send()` function.

And to handle receiving the data you set up a `data_channel.onmessage` handler, just like you set up the `signaling_server.onmessage` handler.

In this way, the core usage of the two API's is almost identical. It is only the underlying network implementation that really differs.

Other file-sharing options

As we have discussed, this example application has focused only on sharing one file at a time and on only sharing image files. Extending this functionality to support multiple files at a time and handling non-image files (for example, documents, videos, and so on) would be a great to start extending this application.

Another option to explore is using typed arrays instead of serialized base64 data URLs to send data. This can work in the same way either through the WebSocket API or the RTCDataChannel API, and can add significant efficiencies.

And of course, if you extend this application to support WebRTC communication between more than just two browsers, then you may also like to extend the file sharing, because you could send a file to just one user by dropping the file onto their video stream or to all users if you drop it into the chat area or file list.

On top of this, you can also use WebSockets and RTCDataChannels for sharing interactive drawing spaces and annotations for creating an interactive whiteboard layer for the application.

Another way is that you could capture snippets of audio and video to share annotations that are like persistent slices of the video call. With this example application you should have everything you need to start implementing your own ideas and have them up and running in no time at all.

Summary

You should now have a clear understanding of how easy it is to adapt our initial video call application to support file sharing. You should be able to update the HTML user interface to add a shared files list. And you should now appreciate even further, how the cleanly abstracted design of the signaling server allows us to easily support new application scenarios.

You should also have all the information you need to start exploring other file sharing options and ideas.

In the final two chapters, we will explore some specific case studies that show how this type of application can be implemented to enable e-learning and team communication.

7
Example Application 1 – Education and E-learning

This chapter maps out what is involved in introducing WebRTC into e-learning applications. It explores the types of components that will be involved in integrating this to create a fully working platform. After reading this chapter, you will have a clear understanding of:

- How WebRTC can be applied in an e-learning context
- How an overall application architecture could be structured
- The types of issues that you may face
- The types of benefits you may realize
- How the overall opportunity can be summarized

Applying WebRTC for education and e-learning

The whole education market is currently undergoing yet another revolution as e-learning platforms such as **Learning Management System (LMS)**, e-portfolios, and **Massive Online Open Course (MOOC)** continue to reshape the whole industry. This has created the perfect fertile ground for the integration of WebRTC. More students and educators are interacting online everyday, but currently this is primarily using standard web page and document-based user interfaces.

The only video and audio conferencing options commonly available to educators and students today are those using proprietary systems, such as Skype, and Adobe Connect. Each of these solutions requires additional software and often a completely standalone application to be installed. The setup time to establish each of these calls is usually quite high, and some of these solutions also require a licensing fee or setup cost.

A recently introduced solution that is gaining quite a bit of attraction in the education and e-learning space is Google Hangouts. Yet, even this requires the download of a proprietary browser plugin and also requires that each participant has an active Google Plus account.

With the introduction of WebRTC, it is now possible to skip all of these setup hurdles and seamlessly add video conferencing, screen sharing, and a whole host of other real-time interaction options to the existing web tools that the educators and students are already using.

By just adding some simple JavaScript and HTML to their existing web pages, these new interaction options can quickly and easily be introduced. And from the end user's perspective, it couldn't be any simpler. They would just see one or two new buttons appearing on their page, and all they have to do is click on them to start a video call, screen sharing session, or more. There is no more installing of applications or plugins and dealing with the complexity of setting up calls.

Overall application architecture

The general architecture for this type of application or platform consists of seven key elements that work together to deliver the overall experience:

- Educators
- Students
- WebRTC capable browsers
- Existing or new web applications
- Signaling server
- TURN server
- Archive server

Let's look at each of these elements in more detail.

Educators

These are the users that drive the creation of the educational content and manage the overall e-learning experience. Many of them have quickly adopted the evolving online tools; however, there are also a large number of them that are struggling with the new technologies and have trouble keeping up with today's high rate of technological change.

When integrated correctly, WebRTC supports both of the early adopters and the not-so-technical educators by making it easy to deliver a state-of-the-art e-learning experience. The early adopters can experiment with new functionality and customize these new tools to their needs. The not-so-technical educators can focus on this as a simple extension of their existing face-to-face teaching delivery.

Students

Like educators, students also consist of both early adopters and not-so-technical users. If they are accessing the web application on campus, then their network access is likely to be relatively fast and reliable. However, many online students participate from home or even work from a wide range of geographical locations where network quality can vary significantly.

The peer-to-peer nature of WebRTC means that the optimal performance is extracted from the available network which increases the chances of a more positive e-learning experience.

WebRTC capable browser

As discussed in *Chapter 1*, *An Introduction to Web-based Real-Time Communication*, Google Chrome and Mozilla Firefox browsers now support the draft, WebRTC 1.0. This is now over 50 percent of the web browser market, and Google claims that this makes WebRTC available to over 1 billion web browsers so far.

However, many educational institutions currently enforce a **Standard Operating Environment (SOE)** internally that limit users to Microsoft Internet Explorer Version 8 or similar. These types of limitations imposed by IT departments may provide one of the biggest hurdles faced by educators trying to take advantage of WebRTC.

Existing or new web application

If students and educators are already using LMSs such as Moodle, ePortfolio systems such as Mahara or MOOCs in general, then these platforms provide the perfect launch pad for connecting these users via WebRTC.

Many educational institutions are also working to create new applications that take advantage of the new web browser and mobile technologies. For example, many institutions now offer "Recognition of Prior Learning" to enable students to earn credits for skills and experience they can clearly demonstrate they already have. This often involves the collection of images and video or audio evidence of them performing some activity. WebRTC can be used to extend this in many ways and is likely to create a whole new type of evidence collection.

Signaling server

As you have seen in the previous chapters, it is relatively straightforward to implement an extensible and lightweight signaling server. In the e-learning context, it is also likely that educational institutions will want to integrate authentication and authorization into this server to provide identity management features and functionality.

TURN server

While WebRTC is built upon the core concept of direct peer-to-peer communication, the current industry experience is that legacy network restrictions may force around 15 percent, and in some cases, even up to 40 percent of users to require a media relay server. The most common solution for this is a **Traversal Using Relays around NAT (TURN)** server. There are a range of commercial and open source options available at `http://code.google.com/p/rfc5766-turn-server/`.

Archive server

There are many different use cases in an e-learning context where recording a copy of a WebRTC video or audio call would be useful or even a hard requirement, due to auditing policies and communication regulations. Recording screen sharing sessions or even other data driven interactions (for example, an interactive whiteboard session) may also be very useful or also required.

This functionality requires a dedicated service that can capture and store WebRTC streams and make them available in an easily findable way. However, the current WebRTC specification does not make this an easy task, and there are currently very few options available for this solution.

Many service providers are developing their own custom archive servers using the open source C++ code base available from `webrtc.org`.

Others are using JavaScript within the browser to capture the stream elements and then sending them via a WebSocket or XHR connection to then be encoded on the server side; however, this is not a network-efficient solution. The still evolving *MediaStream Recording* API available at `http://www.w3.org/TR/2013/WD-mediastream-recording-20130205/` may be useful for browser side developments for archiving.

Potential issues that may be faced

While introducing WebRTC into an e-learning environment, you may find that there are a number of issues that are commonly faced:

- Privacy
- Copyright and intellectual property
- Restrictive networks
- Restrictive SOEs
- Outdated student browsers
- Interoperability

Let's take a look at each of these issues in more detail.

Privacy

Privacy is a key issue facing any video or audio recording application and this issue is made more complex by the distributed nature of the web.

The educational institution providing the e-learning application may have specific privacy policies designed to protect their students; however, it is likely that these policies are out of date and in some cases, may be too restrictive or even prohibit some WebRTC style applications.

The educators employment contracts may also include clauses designed to both protect the educator and to restrict their behavior when it comes to video or audio recording devices. It is important that these restrictions be clearly understood and possibly even reviewed and revised.

The governmental departments that control the overall delivery of education may also impose restrictive privacy policies designed to protect both the educators and students. However, these may also be out of date and in some cases, completely prohibit WebRTC style interactions.

To make this even more complex, users may be bound by different policies or regulations on campus, at home, and at work. It may also happen that in a completely online environment, the educators and students may be in completely separate geographical and legal jurisdictions with wildly differing regulations.

The first and most important step in addressing the complex issue of privacy is to ensure that the capture, handling, and storage of audio, video, and data is managed in a transparent and well-documented way. From there, it is up to each educational institution to address how they will embrace and manage these risks.

It is also important for all educational institutions to understand that this becomes a key part in remaining competitive in the modern education industry and that, if they do not address this issue, then they will be left struggling to provide their most basic services.

Copyright and intellectual property

Recorded video and audio conferences are content in their own right and it is important that the copyright of these works are clearly defined. Many educators may believe that any lessons they deliver are owned by them or their institution. However, in this new environment, this may fall into more of a collaborative codesign model where the final output of a session may be collectively owned.

It is also likely that these video or audio calls and any screen-sharing sessions may also capture other copyright material, such as courseware, webpages, and other content in view of the camera. The intellectual property rights of the owners of this content must be clearly addressed where relevant, and it is important that any recording or archiving solutions allow clear attribution, as well as the ability to easily find and remove or obfuscate copyright material.

Restrictive networks

Both inside and outside the educational institution, there may be restrictive network policies in place that restrict or even prohibit WebRTC style interactions.

IT departments inside educational institutions or work environments often shape network traffic to reduce costs and prevent abuse. Constant streams of data, audio, and video often push these networks beyond the limits they were dimensioned for.

These network administrators have also often implemented firewall restrictions that prevent peers on the same network from communicating with each other to prevent malware and other types of network abuse. In these cases, the connections will need to be routed out through the Internet and back again, often via a media relay server (refer to the *TURN server* section described earlier and in earlier chapters). This effectively removes much of the benefits of the peer-to-peer nature of WebRTC.

In the consumer networks, users may also find that their ISP has provided limits on the speed of data uploads. The normal consumer ISP network design is asymmetrical, and is focused on delivering optimal download speed. However, WebRTC streams such as video calls ship data in both directions and can be heavily impacted by this outdated network design.

If the user is using a mobile network, then it is even more likely that the imposed network policies and embedded proxies limit direct peer-to-peer streams.

However, all of these issues clearly label the impacted network as suffering from outdated "legacy design" issues. All network providers will have to deal with the new requirements of this sensor driven real-time web. Network providers that embrace this challenge and provide superior access will be able to win the loyalty of their users, and in the consumer space, will likely grow their market share and profitability.

Restrictive SOEs

Many educational institutions and corporate work environments have IT departments that enforce a SOE for personal computers. In many cases, this is restricted to older versions of Microsoft Internet Explorer which do not support WebRTC. In this environment, these users will not be able to access these additional features and any e-learning application should detect the browser capabilities and notify the user accordingly (refer to the `webrtc_polyfill.js` code described in previous chapters).

However, all of these institutions and corporations are under pressure to modernize their approach to deliver the benefits made available by up-to-date web browsers.

Many users are also working around these IT department restrictions by bringing their own mobile devices or even laptops (commonly known as **Bring Your Own Device (BYOD)**. This is a significant strategic issue that all IT departments are facing today.

Outdated student browsers

Depending upon the economic and technical profiles of the students, you may also find that their own computers are running an outdated browsers. Again it is important that your e-learning application detects the capabilities of their browser and notifies the user clearly about their upgrade options if they want to take advantage of these new features.

With mobile devices based on iOS and Android, this is becoming less of a problem, because the operating system vendors have built automatic upgrade functionality directly into the core user experience, and you will find that most users are running close to the latest version.

The mainstream browser vendors including Chrome and Firefox have also moved to this automatic update model and users of these browsers are now also more likely to be running close to the latest version. The benefit here is that if you encourage your users to move to these platforms once, then after that the problem is largely handled by the browser vendor from then on. The challenge here is that this then becomes a moving target and automated updates may have an impact on your application in negative ways, if you do not monitor the evolution of these new standards on an ongoing basis.

Interoperability

Although Chrome and Firefox have shown good interoperability based on their rolling version updates, you may find that interoperability still currently varies. During the writing of this book, there were a number of times where previously working examples stopped operating due to updates in one type of browser or another. This is the nature of a pre-WebRTC 1.0 standard, and this is likely to become less and less of an issue as the whole environment stabilizes.

Benefits that can be delivered

While there are still quite a few issues facing the introduction of WebRTC into an e-learning environment, the overall benefits are appealing and significant.

The benefits of the ease of use and removal of barriers for setting up an audio or video call or screen sharing session cannot be underestimated. This will drive more interpersonal interaction between educators and students, among students themselves, and even among educators themselves. This makes the overall e-learning environment more engaging and can lead to better learning outcomes and higher satisfaction levels.

The distributed peer-to-peer nature of WebRTC can also lead to some significant network and infrastructure cost reductions. While some media relay / TURN server infrastructure may be required today, this will be significantly less than using older video conferencing technologies. If you are able to just focus on capable, early adopters initially, then you may be able to skip this cost altogether.

WebRTC is also quickly expanding onto mobile browsers, making it more widely available than traditional video conferencing solutions. This will lead to a wider adoption and make your e-learning platform more accessible and applicable in a wider range of real world situations.

This also opens the door to in situ learner support applications where educators and experts can provide real-time training and support in the work place, creating a whole new class of e-learning applications.

In a similar way, this also opens the door to educator-supported accessibility for visually and cognitively impaired students. By using audio conferencing and data sharing, an educator can guide a student through some specific course content or interaction, significantly improving the overall accessibility.

The JavaScript and HTML driven nature of these WebRTC applications also means that more in-house customization can be implemented within each educational institution, or even by the educators themselves. You are no longer restricted to the look and feel and functionality provided by some distant and unresponsive video conferencing vendor.

And this also means that these applications can be adapted to evolve more quickly to meet the demands of the students and educators. All kinds of new interaction models will be created in e-learning over the next few years, and this is an exciting time to jump in and start implementing your own ideas.

The opportunity for educators

When any landscape changes, new opportunities are created. The introduction of WebRTC-based interactions into the e-learning environment means that educators that adapt to take advantage of this new sensor driven real-time web will be able to engage more closely with their students, achieve better learning outcomes, and naturally advance their personal brand and career. Many educators have embraced similar benefits through social media, now WebRTC is going to make interpersonal and real-time interactions with students seamless and easy.

The key point here is that many educators won't think of this in terms of WebRTC. They will just be able to focus on interacting in richer ways with their students, and exploring new ways of delivering their courseware.

Summary

You should now have a clear understanding of how WebRTC can be implemented into an educational and e-learning context. You should understand the key components that make up this overall application architecture, and how this relates to existing e-learning applications. You should have a good picture of the types of issues you are likely to face while working to implement WebRTC into your e-learning environment. You should also understand the key benefits that will be likely delivered on adding WebRTC to your e-learning applications and the opportunities this will open up for educators who adapt to this new environment.

In the final chapter, we will explore a similar case study that shows how this type of application can be implemented to enable team communication.

8
Example Application 2 – Team Communication

This chapter maps out what is involved in introducing WebRTC into your team communication application. It explores the types of components that will be involved in integrating this to create a fully working platform. After reading this chapter, you will have a clear understanding of:

- How WebRTC can be applied in a team communication context
- How an overall application architecture could be structured
- The types of issues that you may face
- The types of benefits you may realize
- How the overall opportunity can be summarized

Applying WebRTC for team communication

Today, teams form in all kinds of contexts and for all kinds of reasons. Some are commercial teams working inside startups or fully formed companies, or corporations. Some are collaborators within non-profit or social enterprises. And some are contributors to open source projects. Or, they could just be friends or family staying in touch or planning a group event.

The constant now is that all of the team members are very likely to be connected through the web, and many of them are comfortable with popular chat and micro blogging tools, such as Facebook, Twitter, and Google Plus. Team members are now expected to be able to contact each other anywhere, anytime. Participating in one or more distributed teams is now a very normal daily experience.

However, the most common video and audio conferencing options available to managers and team participants are proprietary systems, such as Skype, WebEx, and GoToMeeting. Each of these solutions requires additional software configuration and often a completely standalone application to be installed. The setup time to for each of these calls is also quite high, and the web meeting solutions often require a licensing fee or setup cost.

Just like in the e-learning sector, Google Hangouts are also gaining quite a bit of traction in the team communication space. But, as we have discussed, even this requires the download of a proprietary browser plugin and that each participant has an active Google Plus account.

WebRTC now makes it possible to remove these setup hurdles so that you can seamlessly add video conferencing, screen sharing, and a whole host of other real-time interaction options to bring online teams closer together.

There are already a wide range of new web-based services popping up that are targeting teams, and of course, if you have read this book, then you can easily create your own application too.

In a modern WebRTC-enabled team, you should be able to clearly see who's available at any point in time, and then quickly and easily start talking to them using text or using audio and video by just clicking their photo. No more scheduling meetings or booking web meetings with special access codes is required. And, sharing a file is as simple as dragging it onto their photo in your team list. You can't get much more connected than that!

Overall application architecture

The architecture for this type of application or platform generally consists of seven key elements that work together to deliver the overall experience:

- Managers
- Team members
- WebRTC capable browser
- New and existing web applications
- Signaling server
- TURN server
- Messaging server

Let's look at each of these elements in more detail.

Managers

These are the people that are responsible for bringing the team members together and driving them to achieve a specific set of goals. Managers need to have control of these team applications and be able to add and remove members easily.

They will also want to be able to see information about the activity of each member, and in a business context ideally, also be able to tie these back to key performance indicators so that they can track and manage each individual.

In both a commercial and a non-commercial context, the levels of participation from each of the team members may also be available for all to see, because online teams tend to act more like meritocracy where status is based on performance.

Team members

These are the individuals that are the focus of the team application. They may be distributed all across the globe and connected via all kinds of networks and devices.

The key for these team members is to remove the barriers, so they can communicate as freely as possible. They tend to already have a range of tools they use for tracking their tasks and planning their work. The WebRTC enabled team application is really just there to act as a form of glue, so they can all stay connected and collaborate more easily around the other tools they already use.

WebRTC capable browser

As discussed earlier, Google Chrome and Mozilla Firefox browsers now support the draft WebRTC 1.0. This is now over 50 percent of the web browser market, and Google claims that this makes WebRTC available to over 1 billion web browsers so far.

Many corporate team environments enforce an **SOE** that limits users to older versions of Microsoft Internet Explorer in some cases, such as the Banking and Insurance sectors, this can be as old as Version 6. These limitations imposed by IT departments can provide a significant barrier that can completely block the adoption of WebRTC. However, teams that are already collaborating online tend to be more like early adopters and often use their own laptops and select their own browsers.

Teams in the more social and open environments will almost definitely just be using their own computers or mobile devices and will be able to select their own browser.

New and existing web applications

Most teams today do not tend to have a common web application open all the time. Many use Webmail (for example, Gmail) and a web-based ticketing system. But both of these tend to be provided by external vendors and don't usually allow you to inject new JavaScript and HTML into them easily. Some teams may also use an intranet; although, this is becoming less and less common. So it is likely that you will need to create a new team web app to bring them all together.

The application we developed in *Chapter 5*, *Adding Text-based Chat*, that included video calls, text-based chat, and file sharing can provide a great starting point for creating your own team application.

You will need to add support for more than two participants, and you will also likely want to add support to show their presence or availability. You will probably also want to use predefined hash-based call tokens to define topics or rooms that your team members can join or cluster around instead of the randomly generated call tokens we used.

All of these options are simple extensions of the base application we have already developed. And best of all, you have complete control over the way it works and how it looks. If you or any of your team comes up with new ideas about how it should work, then you can simply update the code to create them yourself. You can even use the application to collaborate with your team on the process of customizing and refining the app itself.

Signaling server

Again, we see here the benefits of the extensible and lightweight signaling server we built in previous chapters. In the team communication context, it is also likely that you will want to integrate some form of authentication and authorization into this server to provide identity management features and functionality. This is also where you are likely to integrate the presence management so you can share information about people's availability. But the underlying structure of the signaling server we have already built should need only minor modifications.

TURN server

As discussed in the e-learning context, WebRTC is built upon the core concept of direct peer-to-peer communication. But the current industry experience is that legacy network restrictions may force approximately 15 percent, and possibly even up to 40 percent of users to require a media relay server.

However, in an online team of early adopters, this rate is likely to be much lower, and you may certainly choose to focus on capable browsers and networks only with a fall, back to text-based chat for other participants.

If you do require a TURN server, then there are a range of commercial and open source options available at `http://code.google.com/p/rfc5766-turn-server/`.

Messaging server

There are a range of features or functionalities that can loosely be described as messaging that you may like to use to extend your team communications. This messaging server may be driven by commands sent through the signaling server, but is likely to be a standalone service on its own.

The types of features you may want this to provide include voice and video mail messages, automated logging of sessions and chat logs, team reminders, time tracking, calendar updates, and general event logging or note taking. The basis of this could start out very similar to the types of "bots" that are commonly developed for **Internet Relay Chat (IRC)** servers. But in many ways, it could also resemble the **Unified Messaging (UM)** or **IP Multimedia Subsystem (IMS)** servers that Telco has been promoting over the last decade. Wherever possible, this should also provide a seamless gateway to your other existing applications and services.

Potential issues that may be faced

When integrating WebRTC into your team-based communication, you are likely to find a number of issues that are commonly faced:

- Privacy
- Data security
- Restrictive networks
- Restrictive SOEs
- Interoperability
- Timezones

Let's take a look at each of these issues in more detail.

Privacy

As in e-learning, privacy is a key issue facing any video or audio recording application within team communications. And as we have discussed, this issue is made more complex by the distributed nature of the web.

In a commercial or organization-based context, the team application may have specific privacy policies enforced. It is possible that these policies are out of date, and, in some cases, may be too restrictive or even prohibit some WebRTC-style applications. But it is equally as likely that no well-structured policies have yet been put in place, which can be just as challenging.

The team members' employment contracts may also include clauses designed to restrict their behavior when it comes to data sharing and possibly using video or audio recording devices. It is important that these restrictions be clearly understood and, where necessary, reviewed and revised.

There may also be government regulations that deal with using recording devices in the workplace, homes, or in public places. These are the same sort of issues that wearable devices including cameras (for example, Google Glass) are currently working to understand.

To make this even more complex, different team members may be bound by different policies or regulations at work, at home, and when they are out and about. Also in a completely online environment, the different team members may be in completely separate geographical and legal jurisdictions with wildly differing regulations.

Because we have discussed previously, the first and most important step in addressing the complex issue of privacy is to ensure that the capture, handling, and storage of audio, video, and data is managed in a transparent and well-documented way. From there, it is up to each team to address how he or she will embrace and manage these risks. This is just part of participating in a modern, efficient, distributed online team.

Data security

As communication and file or data sharing is made so simple by adding WebRTC, it is also possible that private files, data, and other information can then easily be leaked outside the controlled team environment. This can happen inadvertently, or it can be an explicit act by one or more of the team members. This is a similar challenge to that introduced by small USB drives and web-based e-mail within the existing business environment.

It is important that clear data security policies are in place and that where necessary secure transport protocols (for example, SSL or TLS) are used for all WebSocket and WebRTC data exhanges.

This is not the case with the current demonstration applications from this book.

It is also important that these policies and practices are clearly understood by all the team members, and that a culture of secure data handling is built into the team from the ground itself.

Restrictive networks

At any point, there may be restrictive network policies applied that restrict or even prohibit WebRTC-style interactions.

IT departments inside companies or corporations tend to shape network traffic to reduce costs and prevent abuse. Constant streams of data, audio, and video often push these networks beyond the limits for which they were designed.

Network administrators also tend to implement firewall restrictions that prevent peers on the same network communicating with each other to prevent malware and other types of network abuse. In these cases, the connections may need to be routed out through the internet and back again via a media relay server (refer to the *TURN server* section described before and in earlier chapters). This removes the benefits of the peer-to-peer nature of WebRTC.

In the consumer network space, users may also find that their ISP has provided limits on the speed of data uploads. Consumer ISP networks are designed to be asymmetrical and are focused on delivering optimal download speeds. However, WebRTC streams, such as video calls, ship data in both directions and are heavily restricted by this outdated network design.

If any of the team members are using a mobile network, then it is even more likely that the imposed network policies and embedded proxies could limit direct peer-to-peer streams.

All of these issues position the impacted network as suffering from an outdated "legacy design". All network providers will have to deal with the new requirements of this sensor-driven, real-time web. Network providers that embrace this challenge and provide superior access will then be able to win the loyalty of their users, and in the consumer space, will likely grow their market share and profitability.

Restrictive SOEs

Corporate work environments often have IT departments that enforce a SOE for personal computers. In many cases, this is restricted to older versions of Microsoft Internet Explorer which do not support WebRTC.

In this type of environment, these users will not be able to access the added WebRTC features at all. This means it is essential that your team communication application should detect the browser capabilities and notify the user accordingly (refer to the `webrtc_polyfill.js` code described in previous chapters).

Yet, all of these corporate IT departments are already under pressure to modernize their approach, so they can unlock the benefits made available by up-to-date web browsers.

Many team members also work around these IT department restrictions by bringing their own mobile devices or even laptops (BYOD). This is a significant strategic issue that all IT departments are facing today, and is likely to be even more common among early adopters that work in online teams.

Interoperability

As we have discussed earlier, Chrome and Firefox have shown good interoperability. But based on their rolling version updates, you are likely to find that interoperability still currently varies. During the writing of this book, there were a number of times where previously working examples stopped working because updates in one type of browser or another had impacted them negatively. Unfortunately, this is the nature of a pre-WebRTC 1.0 standard, and this is likely to become less of an issue as the whole environment stabilizes.

Timezones

As teams become more geographically distributed, you may also find timezones becoming a significant hurdle that you must handle. The sun is constantly rising somewhere in the world, and ensuring that key team members are all available at important times is critical. This is not specifically a WebRTC issue, but just part of the challenge of running a distributed online team. Ironically, the best way to deal with this issue is to ensure that there is open and clear communication within the team about this. And this is exactly what WebRTC helps to enable.

Benefits that can be delivered

Team communication can be one of the best environments to benefit from the early introduction of WebRTC.

By streamlining communication, removing the barriers for setting up an audio or video call, or screen sharing session, you can completely reshape the way your team works. You can drive more interpersonal interaction among the whole team.

The distributed peer-to-peer nature of WebRTC can also lead to significant network and infrastructure cost reductions. While some TURN server infrastructure may be required today, this will be significantly less than using older video conferencing technologies, where web or video conference vendors were required. And, if you are able to focus on capable, early adopters initially, then you may be able to skip this cost altogether.

WebRTC is also quickly expanding onto mobile browsers, making it more widely available than traditional video conferencing solutions. This will lead to a wider adoption and gets the team connected and communicating no matter where they are. If any of your team is out in the field, then this alone can revolutionize how you all work.

This also opens the door to infield support applications, where team members can collaborate in real-time in the locations where it's most relevant. Your team expert can help guide your field service engineers to solve technical issues. Or your manager may help your sales staff resolve an issue or close a contract with a key customer. Or your domain expert may help your volunteers collect plant specimens or crucial data from an important location. The distance between all of your team members has now collapsed, and the friction of legacy communication systems can now be removed.

The JavaScript- and HTML-driven nature of these WebRTC applications also means that more in-house customization can be implemented. Possibly even the team members themselves can adapt and change the application. You are no longer restricted to the look and feel and functionality provided by some distant and unresponsive solution provider.

This also means that these applications can be adapted to evolve more quickly to meet the demands of the whole team. You now have the tools to build exactly the type of communication platform you need.

The opportunity for managers

Communication is the lifeblood of any modern team, and WebRTC is reshaping the communication landscape all around us. This is creating all kinds of new opportunities, and the managers that help their teams take advantage of this new sensor driven real-time web will be able achieve more, and advance their personal careers. Many teams have struggled to adapt to the new world of social media. Now, WebRTC is going to make the world inside your team even more like a rich social media space and the managers that adapt to this will be the leaders of tomorrow.

If you focus on the social, cultural, and interpersonal aspects of this new environment, and work to create a team communication application that seamlessly connects your team members, then you will be able to create a whole new generation of highly performing teams.

To start with, don't focus on building all kinds of features and functionality into the application. It is easy to get distracted by focusing on the tools themselves. What is most important is that the user experience is simple and effective, and that team members quickly integrate it into their daily activities. From there you can expand the application as much as you like. But without this, focusing on features is purely a distraction.

Summary

You should now have a clear understanding of how WebRTC can be integrated into a team communication application. You should understand the key components that make up this overall application architecture and how this enables you to create a new type of team web application. You should have a good picture of the types of issues you are likely to face while working to implement WebRTC into your team communication. You should also understand the key benefits of adding WebRTC to your team communication application will likely deliver, and the opportunities this will open for managers and teams as a whole as they adapt to this new environment.

This completes our *Getting Started with WebRTC* journey. Now, you should be well-equipped to start creating your own WebRTC applications and implementing your own ideas. I hope you enjoyed reading this book and found the demonstration code clear and the example application discussions useful.

Index

H

HTML user interface, audio only calls 48
HTML user interface, for file sharing 60, 61
HTML user interface, for text-based
       chat 54, 55
http_server variable 37

I

ICE Framework
  reference link 17
intellectual property 80
Internet Engineering Task Force (IETF) 8
Internet Relay Chat (IRC)
  about 57
  servers 89
interoperability 82, 92
IP Multimedia Subsystem (IMS) 89

J

JavaScript
  adding, for file sharing via
      WebSockets 66-68
  adding, to enable file sharing 62
JavaScript functions
  adding, to enable chatting 56
JSON.parse() method 38

L

Learning Management System (LMS) 75
listen() function 37
local video streams
  previewing 42
log_comment function 40
log_error function 40

M

managers
  about 87
  opportunities 94
Massive Online Open Course (MOOC) 75
MediaElement 20
MediaStream API 19, 20

MediaStream Recording
  URL 78
messaging server 89
Microsoft
  about 12
  WebRTC, enabling 12

N

NAT Traversal
  reference link 17
Node.js
  about 18
  URL 26

O

onload function 70
Opera
  about 11
  WebRTC, enabling 11
outdated student browsers 81

P

peer_connection variable 30
peer-to-peer streams
  establishing 43
privacy 79, 90
progress updates
  providing 71, 72

R

readAsDataURL() function 65
restrictive networks 80, 91
restrictive SOEs 81, 92
RTCDataChannel API 23
RTCDataChannel connection
  establishing 72
  files, transfering 72
RTCPeerConnection API
  about 20
  callee's flow 21
  caller's flow 20
  location 23
RTCPeerConnection streams 18

Thank you for buying
Getting Started with WebRTC

About Packt Publishing

Packt, pronounced 'packed', published its first book "*Mastering phpMyAdmin for Effective MySQL Management*" in April 2004 and subsequently continued to specialize in publishing highly focused books on specific technologies and solutions.

Our books and publications share the experiences of your fellow IT professionals in adapting and customizing today's systems, applications, and frameworks. Our solution based books give you the knowledge and power to customize the software and technologies you're using to get the job done. Packt books are more specific and less general than the IT books you have seen in the past. Our unique business model allows us to bring you more focused information, giving you more of what you need to know, and less of what you don't.

Packt is a modern, yet unique publishing company, which focuses on producing quality, cutting-edge books for communities of developers, administrators, and newbies alike. For more information, please visit our website: www.packtpub.com.

About Packt Open Source

In 2010, Packt launched two new brands, Packt Open Source and Packt Enterprise, in order to continue its focus on specialization. This book is part of the Packt Open Source brand, home to books published on software built around Open Source licences, and offering information to anybody from advanced developers to budding web designers. The Open Source brand also runs Packt's Open Source Royalty Scheme, by which Packt gives a royalty to each Open Source project about whose software a book is sold.

Writing for Packt

We welcome all inquiries from people who are interested in authoring. Book proposals should be sent to author@packtpub.com. If your book idea is still at an early stage and you would like to discuss it first before writing a formal book proposal, contact us; one of our commissioning editors will get in touch with you.

We're not just looking for published authors; if you have strong technical skills but no writing experience, our experienced editors can help you develop a writing career, or simply get some additional reward for your expertise.

Microsoft Lync 2013 Unified Communications: From Telephony to Real-time Communication in the Digital Age

ISBN: 978-1-84968-506-1   Paperback: 224 pages

Complete coverage of all topics for a unified communications strategy

1. A real business case and example project showing you how you can optimize costs and improve your competitive advantage with a Unified Communications project

2. The book combines both business and the latest relevant technical information so it is a great reference for business stakeholders, IT decision makers, and UC technical experts

3. All that you need to know about Unified Communications and the evolution of telecommunications is packed in this book

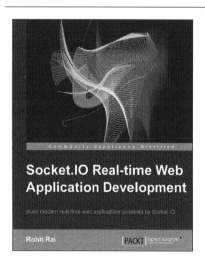

Socket.IO Real-time Web Application Development

ISBN: 978-1-78216-078-6   Paperback: 140 pages

Build modern real-time web applications powered by Socket.IO

1. Understand the usage of various socket.io features like rooms, namespaces, and sessions

2. Secure the socket.io communication

3. Deploy and scale your socket.io and Node.js applications in production

Please check **www.PacktPub.com** for information on our titles

Ext JS 4 Web Application Development Cookbook

ISBN: 978-1-84951-686-0   Paperback: 488 pages

Over 110 easy-to-follow recipes backed up with real-life examples, walking you through basic Ext JS features to advanced application design using Sencha's Ext JS

1. Learn how to build Rich Internet Applications with the latest version of the Ext JS framework in a cookbook style

2. From creating forms to theming your interface, you will learn the building blocks for developing the perfect web application

3. Easy to follow recipes step through practical and detailed examples which are all fully backed up with code, illustrations, and tips

IBM Lotus Quickr 8.5 for Domino Administration

ISBN: 978-1-84968-052-3   Paperback: 252 pages

Ensure effective and efficient team collaboration by building a solid social infrastructure with IBM Lotus Quickr 8.5

1. Gain a thorough understanding of IBM Lotus Quickr 8.5 Team Collaboration, Repository, and Connectors

2. Recommended best practices to upgrade to the latest version of IBM Lotus Quickr 8.5

3. Customize logos, colors, templates, and more to your designs without much effort

Please check **www.PacktPub.com** for information on our titles

Made in the USA
San Bernardino, CA
24 April 2014